The Royal Commission on
Historical Manuscripts

Accessions to Repositories

and Reports added to the
National Register of Archives

1987

D0318041

London: Her Majesty's
Stationery Office

c

Contents

Preface

The aim of *Accessions to Repositories* is
to provide historians with concise
descriptions of the more important or
unusual accessions to record
repositories in the British Isles during
the past year. Information about
routine accessions must be sought
from the repositories themselves or
their published reports.

The Commission is again grateful to
all those who respond to its annual
request for information. Contributions
from 184 repositories have been
included in Part I of this year's issue. It
has been edited for press by NW
James, assisted by Wendy Goldsmith
and AR Smith.

Part II contains the usual list of
numbered reports added to the
National Register of Archives during
the year. In July 1987 new reports
began to be registered on-line by
means of the Commission's computer.

BS SMITH
Secretary

*Quality House, Quality Court,
Chancery Lane, London WC2A 1HP*

Note on access

The inclusion of material in Part I of this
publication does not necessarily imply
that it is yet available for research.
Enquiries about access should in all cases
be directed to the relevant repositories.

I: Accessions to Repositories

National and Special Repositories

ABERDEEN UNIVERSITY

UNIVERSITY LIBRARY, KING'S COLLEGE,
ABERDEEN AB9 2UB

Irvine family of Drum: further corresp
and papers 1716–44

Henry Hamilton, economic historian:
working papers rel to the *Third Statistical
Account of Scotland* c1960

James Francis Edward Keith
(1696–1758), Marshal Keith: personal
and family papers 18th–19th cent

Robert Laws (1851–1934), missionary:
papers

Robert Douglas Lockhart (1894–1987),
professor of anatomy: papers

American Society for Archaeological
Research in Asia Minor: records of
expeditions 20th cent

BIRMINGHAM UNIVERSITY

UNIVERSITY LIBRARY, PO BOX 363,
BIRMINGHAM B15 2TT

Robert Anthony Eden (1897–1977), 1st
Earl of Avon: further personal and
political papers

Chamberlain family of Birmingham
(addnl): autograph letters

BRISTOL UNIVERSITY

UNIVERSITY LIBRARY, TYNDALL AVENUE,
BRISTOL BS8 1TJ

Western Counties Liberal Federation
records 1927–67

THEATRE COLLECTION, DEPARTMENT OF
DRAMA, 29 PARK ROW, BRISTOL BS1 5LT

Sir Herbert Beerbohm Tree (1852–1917),
actor-manager and Maud, Lady Tree
(1864–1937), actress: further corresp and
misc papers

Olivia Truman (1888–1970), author:
corresp and misc papers, incl letters from
Sir Herbert Beerbohm Tree

Old Vic Theatre, London: further
records (transferred from the Theatre
Museum, London)

BRITISH ARCHITECTURAL LIBRARY

ROYAL INSTITUTE OF BRITISH
ARCHITECTS, 66 PORTLAND PLACE,
LONDON W1N 4AD

David Du R Aberdeen & Partners,
architects, London: records 1934–85

Martin Shaw Briggs (1882–1977):
drawings and papers

Ralph Erskine: papers rel to Byker
housing scheme, Newcastle upon
Tyne, 1968–82

David Barclay Niven: papers 1889–1935

Percy William Pocock: drawings and
papers 1896–1952

Robert Weir Schultz: drawings and
papers 1879–1948

Modular Society Ltd: records 1953–76

BRITISH LIBRARY

DEPARTMENT OF WESTERN
MANUSCRIPTS, BRITISH LIBRARY,
GREAT RUSSELL STREET,
LONDON WC1B 3DG

Ferdinand II, King of Aragon: letters rel
to the participation of Henry VIII in the
Holy League 1511 (Add Ch 76634)

Nicholas Charles, Lancaster herald:
further pedigrees from visitations of
Devon, Dorset and Suffolk c1606
(Add MS 64128)

Parliamentary journal 1641–42,
attributed to Thomas Standish MP
(Add MS 64807)

Pelham family, Earls of Chichester:
further family corresp and papers
1738–1922, incl corresp of Thomas
Pelham Holles, Duke of Newcastle
1738–68 (Add MS 64813)

Revolution Society: minute book
1788–91 (Add MS 64814)

Henrietta Antonia Clive, Countess of
Powis: corresp and papers 1792–1823
(Add MS 64105)

Arthur Wellesley, 1st Duke of
Wellington: letters, papers and
despatches of and rel to him 1809–14
(Add MS 64131)

Charles Sturge (1800–88), Quaker
businessman and politician: personal and
family corresp, incl letters from Henry
Ashworth, Jacob and John Bright and
George Wilson (Add MS 64130)

William Booth (1829–1912) and
Catherine Booth (1829–90), founders of
the Salvation Army: corresp and papers
(Add MSS 64799–64806)

Sir Francis Ottiwell Adams, diplomat:
letter book as minister *ad interim* to
France 1878–81 (Add MS 64796)

*Photographic copies of exported MSS
acquired through the Department of Trade
under the export licensing regulations and
which became available for use during 1987
include the following:*

Vice-Admiral William Bligh: charts and
papers rel to his voyage to Timor 1789
(RP 1927)

Lt-General Sir Henry Edward Bunbury,
7th Bt: memoir rel to the defence of Sicily
1806 (RP 1921)

Jane, Lady Franklin: letters 1850–51 etc
(RP 1868)

Florence Nightingale: letters to JS Mill,
CP Villiers and the Parkinson family
1860–67 (RP 2027–28)

INDIA OFFICE LIBRARY AND RECORDS,
197 BLACKFRIARS ROAD, LONDON SE1 8NG

Captain Charles Marsh, 84th Regt:
letters and papers c1761–87,
incl regimental order book 1763–64

JP Scott: account book of commercial
activities in India 1777–86

Major-General William Kirkpatrick
(1754–1812) and Lt-Colonel James
Achilles Kirkpatrick (1764–1805),
residents at Hyderabad: further
corresp and papers (transferred
from Somerset RO)

Captain William Hambly, East India Co
Maritime Service: account book rel to his
trading interests 1780–84

James Edward Fitzgerald, prime minister
of New Zealand, and Captain Robert
Fitzgerald, Sind Camel Corps: corresp
and papers 1835–81

Shapurji Saklatvala (1874–1936) MP:
letters and papers

Sir Edward Penderel Moon (*b*1905), Indian administrator and historian: further corresp and papers

Royal Society for India, Pakistan and Ceylon (addnl): India Society minute book 1910–24

Indian Political Service: memoirs of former members and their wives *c*1920–47

BRITISH MUSEUM
(NATURAL HISTORY)

CROMWELL ROAD, LONDON SW7 5BD

Leslie Beeching Hall, botanist: diaries and papers 1901–38

Charles Carmichael Lacaita, botanist (addnl): corresp and papers *c*1910–25

Percy Roycroft Lowe (1870–1948), ornithologist: corresp

Frank Ludlow (1885–1972), botanist (addnl): corresp and papers

Richard Meinertzhagen (1878–1967), ornithologist (addnl): working papers and drawings

John William Salter, geologist (addnl): corresp and family papers *c*1835–85

Daniel Carlsson Solander, botanist (addnl): descriptions of fish and other animals from Cook's first voyage 1768–71

Dawson Turner, botanist (addnl): letters (10) to James and James de Carle Sowerby 1798–1816

George Charles Wallich, biologist (addnl): diaries, corresp and papers *c*1850–70

Medico-Botanical Society of London (addnl): records 1824–39

Ray Society minutes 1844–1948

CAMBRIDGE UNIVERSITY

DEPARTMENT OF MANUSCRIPTS, UNIVERSITY LIBRARY, WEST ROAD, CAMBRIDGE CB3 9DR

Thomas Brand, chancellor of Lincoln Cathedral: letters rel to his European travels 1779–93

George Parker Bidder (1863–1953), marine biologist: personal and family papers

Sir Charles Villiers Stanford, composer: notes at Bayreuth Festival 1876

JPT Bury (1908–1987), historian: corresp

John Smart, entomologist: letters from N America 1932–53

John Cowper Powys and Littleton Charles Powys, authors: letters to Ichiro Hara 1952–62

UNIVERSITY ARCHIVES, UNIVERSITY LIBRARY, WEST ROAD, CAMBRIDGE CB3 9DR

Sir John Cowdery Kendrew, molecular biologist: misc papers 1969–86

Cambridge University Press: further records *c*1870–1980

CHURCHILL COLLEGE, CAMBRIDGE CB3 0DS

Sir Richard Clarke (1910–75), civil servant: corresp and papers

Sir Eric Eastwood (1910–81), engineer: corresp and papers rel to research on radar

Sir James Wycliffe Headlam-Morley (1863–1929), civil servant: corresp and papers

Sir Alan Frederick Lascelles (1887–1982), private secretary to George VI: diaries and papers

Sir Frank Cavendish Lascelles (1841–1920), diplomat (addnl): letters and diaries

Sir Denys Wilkinson (b1922), nuclear physicist: corresp and papers

TRINITY COLLEGE LIBRARY,
CAMBRIDGE CB2 1TQ

Walter Thomas Layton (1884–1966), 1st Baron Layton (addnl): family papers

George Edward Moore, philosopher: letters (15) to Norman Malcolm 1941–58

Ludwig Wittgenstein, philosopher: letters (57) to Norman Malcolm 1940–51

Sylvia Goodfellow, private secretary to Richard Austen Butler, Baron Butler: diary 1941–45

CHURCH OF IRELAND

REPRESENTATIVE CHURCH BODY
LIBRARY, BRAEMOR PARK, RATHGAR,
DUBLIN 14

Euseby Cleaver, archbishop of Dublin (addnl): family corresp and papers 1789–1939

Edward Synge, bishop of Elphin: letters 1760–61

Incorporated Society for Promoting Protestant Schools in Ireland: further estate papers 19th cent

Monkstown Clerical Union, co Dublin: minute books 1861–1957

Protestant Orphan Society, co Sligo: records 1839–1984

DUBLIN UNIVERSITY

TRINITY COLLEGE LIBRARY, COLLEGE
STREET, DUBLIN 2

Campbell family of co Antrim: letters from N America 1796–1851

Wynne family of Hazlewood, co Sligo: papers 18th–20th cent

William Alcock, colonel in the Waterford militia: journal 1761–62

DUNDEE UNIVERSITY

UNIVERSITY LIBRARY, DUNDEE DD1 4HN

Lewis C Grant & Co Ltd, machinery mfrs, Dysart: further records c1846–1960

H & A Scott Ltd, polypropylene and jute goods mfrs, Dundee: records 1880–1985

Scottish Co-operative Wholesale Society Ltd, jute goods mfrs, Dundee: records 1966–83

Dundee Royal Infirmary (addnl): records 1839–1971

Sidlaw Sanatorium, Auchterhouse: minutes 1899–1910

DURHAM UNIVERSITY

UNIVERSITY LIBRARY, PALACE GREEN,
DURHAM DH1 3RN

The Poor Caitiff c1400

Howlett family corresp and papers, incl papers rel to Samuel Burt Howlett (1794–1874), surveyor and inventor

Robert Surtees (1779–1834), antiquary and topographer: further working papers

Spennymoor settlement records c1930–59

DEPARTMENT OF PALAEOGRAPHY AND
DIPLOMATIC, THE PRIOR'S KITCHEN,
THE COLLEGE, DURHAM DH1 3EQ

Durham diocese: further papers, incl corresp and misc papers of bishops JB Lightfoot c1879–89 and BF Westcott c1852–1900 and corresp of HH Henson c1920–39 and ATP Williams c1940–51

Grey family, Earls Grey: further estate papers 19th–20th cent

GLASGOW UNIVERSITY

THE LIBRARY, HILLHEAD STREET,
GLASGOW G12 8QE

James Pittendrigh Macgillivray
(1856–1938), sculptor: misc corresp

UNIVERSITY ARCHIVES, THE UNIVERSITY,
GLASGOW G12 8QQ

Ross Wilson (b1914), author: papers

William Collins, Sons & Co Ltd,
publishers, Glasgow: records 1822–1984

W Grant & Co, wood pulp agents,
Edinburgh: records 1880–1971

David & William Henderson & Co Ltd,
shipbuilders, Glasgow: records 1854–99,
incl Tod & McGregor, shipbuilders,
1854–73

A Kirkpatrick & Sons Ltd, provision
merchants and dealers, Glasgow: records
1888–1960

John Laird & Son Ltd, packaging mfrs,
Glasgow: records 1929–81

Marshall, Fleming & Co Ltd, crane mfrs,
Motherwell: records 1890–1981

James Marshall (Glasgow) Ltd, macaroni
and semolina mfrs: records 1886–1982

John Stewart & Co (Wishaw) Ltd, motor
body builders: records 1936–79

Burmah Shareholders Action Group
records 1972–85

Royal Scottish Academy of Music and
Drama records 1870–1985

HISTORY OF ADVERTISING TRUST

202 BUTLERS WHARF BUSINESS CENTRE,
54 CURLEW STREET, LONDON SE1 2ND

RF White & Son Ltd, advertising agents,
London: records 1790–1980

Advertising Creative Circle records
1951–83

Association of Independent Radio
Contractors Ltd: records 1973–83

British Direct Marketing Association
records 1929–79

Institute of Public Relations records
1946–83

National Dairy Council records 1920–84

Solus Outdoor Advertising Association
records 1938–84

HOUSE OF LORDS

RECORD OFFICE, HOUSE OF LORDS,
LONDON SW1A 0PW

Braye (Browne) MSS: further papers
c1510–1665, incl House of Commons
diaries 1593, 1601, and House of Lords
draft journal 1641–42

House of Commons diary Feb 1663,
Jan–Feb 1667

Sir Clive Morrison-Bell Bt, MP (addnl):
diaries 1903–56

HULL UNIVERSITY

BRYNMOR JONES LIBRARY,
THE UNIVERSITY, HULL HU6 7RX

Maurice Warwick Beresford, historian:
working papers c1968–75

Douglas Eaglesham Dunn, author:
further papers, incl letters from Philip
Larkin 1968–85

Walter Greendale, trade unionist: further
papers c1970–79

IMPERIAL WAR MUSEUM

DEPARTMENT OF DOCUMENTS,
IMPERIAL WAR MUSEUM, LAMBETH ROAD,
LONDON SE1 6HZ

Captain Frank H Alderson: diary as a
midshipman in HMS *Lion* 1914–15

Major-General Ronald FK Belchem: further papers, incl letters from Viscount Montgomery 1944–70

Lt-Colonel GA Cardew: papers rel to service with Royal Field Artillery 1914–19

Brigadier EEE Cass: papers 1940–44

Lt-Colonel CP Dawnay: papers 1940–67, incl letters from Viscount Montgomery

Brigadier CE de Wolff: memoir of his military career 1914–45

Sir Patrick Duff, civil servant: letters rel to his service at Gallipoli 1915

General Sir Alexander John Godley: letters to him rel to the Curragh incident 1914

Major-General Leonard Arthur Hawes (1892–1986): autobiography and papers

Major-General Sir John EW Headlam: papers rel to his service in the Boer and First World Wars

Air Commodore JMD Ker: flying log books 1929–59

Lt-General Sir Oliver WH Leese: papers rel to war service c1914–45

Colonel CRW Norman: letters rel to his military service 1934–59

Squadron-Leader Hugh Quinlan: papers as governor of Spandau prison etc 1945–47

Major MAW Rose: diaries as a signaller 1939–46

Vice-Admiral Sir Charles EB Simeon: papers rel to his command of HMS *Renown* 1939–41

Air Vice Marshal Sturley Philip Simpson: flying log books 1915–16, 1931–34

General Sir Horace Lockwood Smith-Dorrien (addnl): papers 1879–1930

Colonel RG Turner: letters as a liaison officer in Russia etc 1942–46

Brigadier Arthur Bowen van Straubenzee: letters rel to his service in S Africa 1911–12 and France 1915–18

Air Vice Marshal Brian Courtney Yarde: papers rel to the Berlin airlift etc 1948–57

INSTITUTION OF CIVIL ENGINEERS

1–7 GREAT GEORGE STREET, LONDON SW1P 3AA

Thomas Townshend, railway engineer, Smethwick: papers 1826–43

George Raymond Brueton, consulting engineer: papers rel to accidents in construction and allied industries 1969–85

INSTITUTION OF ELECTRICAL ENGINEERS

SAVOY PLACE, LONDON WC2R 0BL

Taplow Court Technical Society records 1949–87

Womens Engineering Society records 1919–79

LAMBETH PALACE LIBRARY

LONDON SE1 7JU

Parish records of Holy Trinity, Minories, London 1566–1686

Lionel Cranfield, 1st Earl of Middlesex: household book 1622

Michael Solomon Alexander (1799–1845), bishop in Jerusalem: papers

Sidney Leslie Ollard (1875–1949), historian: papers

Church of England Mens Society records 1899–1986

LEEDS UNIVERSITY

BROTHERTON LIBRARY,
UNIVERSITY OF LEEDS, LEEDS LS2 9JT

Paget family, baronets, of Cranmore, Somerset: family letters and papers 1882–1981

John Kitching of Darlington, Quaker: commonplace book 1790–92

Sir Henry Legge-Bourke (1914–73) MP: corresp and papers

Association of Education Committees: records 1919–75

LIVERPOOL UNIVERSITY

SYDNEY JONES LIBRARY, UNIVERSITY
LIBRARY, LIVERPOOL L69 3DA

Rathbone family: further family corresp and papers 1798–1947, incl misc corresp and papers of Eleanor Florence Rathbone MP 1930–47

Augustine Birrell (1850–1933), author and statesman: further corresp and misc papers

Felicia Dorothea Hemans, poet: MS poem 'Gertrude' and further letters c1825–27

Joseph Mayer (1803–86), antiquary: corresp and papers rel to *Sprott's Chronicle*

John Sampson (1862–1931), Romani scholar: corresp and papers

William Olaf Stapledon (1886–1950), philosopher: further papers

UNIVERSITY ARCHIVES, PO BOX 147,
LIVERPOOL L69 3BX

Morys GL Bruce, 4th Baron Aberdare: papers rel to history of tennis and rackets c1950–85

Sir Cyril Lodowic Burt, psychologist: further papers 1958–71

Leslie Spencer Hearnshaw, psychologist: working papers 1932–85

Thomas Spensley Simey, Baron Simey (1906–69), social scientist: papers

LONDON UNIVERSITY

UNIVERSITY OF LONDON LIBRARY,
SENATE HOUSE, MALET STREET,
LONDON WC1 7HU

Samuel Wilderspin (c1792–1866), pioneer of infant schools: papers

BRITISH LIBRARY OF POLITICAL AND
ECONOMIC SCIENCE,
10 PORTUGAL STREET, LONDON WC2A 2HD

Philip WS Andrews (d1971) and Elizabeth Brunner (1920–83), economists: corresp and papers

Arthur George Bottomley, Baron Bottomley: papers rel to former colonies c1970–79

James Callaghan (b1912), Baron Callaghan: papers

Evan FM Durbin (1906–48), MP and economist: corresp and papers

Albany Trust records c1960–87

International Year of Peace 1986: records 1985–87

Liberal Party records c1924–82

IMPERIAL COLLEGE OF SCIENCE AND
TECHNOLOGY, LONDON SW7 2AZ

Bernard Hunt, mining engineer: diaries rel to Peru 1896–99

KING'S COLLEGE LONDON ARCHIVES,
STRAND, LONDON WC2R 2LS

Julian Brown (1923–1987), palaeographer: corresp and papers

Donald Holroyd Hey, chemist (addnl): corresp rel to the discovery of free radicals 1936–37

Modern Poetry in Translation records 1965–83

Captain JG Burton: papers rel to the invasion of Italy 1943

Colonel RD Cribb: papers 1918–57

Admiral Bernard Currey: papers 1876–1915

Brigadier Sydney Thomas Divers: papers, mainly rel to N Africa and Italy 1942–45

Wing Commander EPM Fernbank: flying log books 1938–44

Major-General Charles Howard Foulkes (1875–1969): further papers

General Sir Alexander John Godley: corresp 1901–54

Air Vice Marshal Stewart WB Menaul: papers 1955–86

Lt Commander TL Metters: journal of operations against Turkish nationalists etc 1919–20

Brigadier EJ Paton Walsh: papers 1895–1947

Lt-Colonel VEO Stevenson-Hamilton: papers 1940–73 mainly rel to the Gurkhas in Burma

Major-General Percival Napier White: papers rel to SHAPE 1953–57

Sir Chaloner Grenville Alabaster, consul-general at Canton: diaries and misc papers 1854–98

Arnold Adriaan Baké, Sanskrit scholar: papers rel to Indian music c1926–56

James Legge, missionary and sinologist: letters and papers 1860–97

Ifor Ball Powell, historian: papers c1928–85

George Caley, botanist: travel diary 1811–17

David Hannay, journalist and naval historian (addnl): diaries and notebooks 1852–80, incl those of James Hannay (1827–73), journalist

Stanley Victor Keeling, philosopher: corresp and papers 1934–71

Rudolf Olden, writer on German history (addnl): letters to Peter Olden etc 1935–36

University College Union Debating Society records 1855–1969

MANCHESTER UNIVERSITY

Arden family, Barons Alvanley (addnl): estate papers 1797–1851

Leigh family of West Hall, High Legh, Cheshire: legal papers 1717–1874

Leycester family of Toft, Cheshire: further estate papers 18th–19th cent

Joseph Barlow Brooks (1874–1952), Methodist minister: personal and family corresp and papers

Frederick Hunter (1902–77), Methodist minister: corresp and papers

Thomas Russell (1806–89), primitive Methodist preacher: corresp rel to him

NATIONAL ARMY MUSEUM

ROYAL HOSPITAL ROAD, LONDON SW3 4HT

Lt-General John Adlercron: journals c1752–59

Captain Alexander Topham, Somerset militia: order book 1779

Field-Marshal Sir William Maynard Gomm: papers 1840–65

Captain George William Wright, Bengal engineers: engineering notebook and diary of siege of Lucknow 1857

Lt-General Sir Gerald Francis Ellison (1861–1947): corresp and papers

Major-General Charles Edward Lawrie (1864–1953): further diaries and papers

Major-General Bertram Reveley Mitford: diaries rel to Hong Kong and the Sudan 1883–96

General Sir Augustus FAN Thorne (1885–1970): papers

Captain William EL Stewart, mounted infantry: letters from S Africa 1899–1902

Captain Charles Boswell Norman, writer on military affairs: working papers 1910–19

Major John Harper-Nelson, Somaliland Scouts and King's African Rifles: papers 1953–61

NATIONAL LIBRARY OF IRELAND

KILDARE STREET, DUBLIN 2

Armstrong family of Moyaliffe, co Tipperary: family and estate papers 18th–20th cent

Balfour family of Townley Hall, co Louth: further family and estate papers 18th–19th cent

Shackleton family of Ballitore, co Kildare (addnl): corresp c1710–1843

Roger David Casement (1864–1916), nationalist: further corresp

George Noble Plunkett (1851–1948), politician and Joseph Mary Plunkett (1887–1916), poet and nationalist: further papers

Valentine EP MacSwiney (1871–1945), papal diplomat: papers

NATIONAL LIBRARY OF SCOTLAND

DEPARTMENT OF MANUSCRIPTS,
NATIONAL LIBRARY OF SCOTLAND,
GEORGE IV BRIDGE, EDINBURGH EH1 1EW

Boyd family, publishers, Edinburgh: papers c1750–1950

Irvine family of Drum, Aberdeenshire: further corresp and papers 1762–1843

Menzies family, baronets, of Menzies, Perthshire: further papers 1690–1821

Robert Adam, architect: papers rel to Edinburgh South Bridge 1785–89

William Barclay (1907–1978), New Testament scholar: corresp and papers

John Brown (1754–1832), minister of the Burgher Church, Whitburn: papers

Robert Burns, poet: further corresp and papers of and rel to him c1780–96

John Cairns, theologian and philosopher (addnl): corresp c1830–80

James Naughton Dandie (1894–1976), solicitor: letters from France 1914–19

William Douglas-Home, playwright: corresp and papers 1936–87

Robert Purves Hardie (1864–1942), writer on fishing (addnl): papers 1900–40

David Hume, philosopher and historian (addnl): corresp and papers 1727–76

James Miller (1893–1987), artist: corresp and papers

Sir George Taylor, botanist: corresp and papers 1919–87

Nigel Godwin Tranter, author: further corresp and papers 1950–86

James Dickson & Co, wholesale stationers, Edinburgh: records 1818–1932

Gairm Publications, Glasgow: editorial corresp and papers 1952–85

Kelso Races Ltd records 1812–1962

JG Thomson & Co Ltd, wine and spirit merchants, Leith: records 1786–1981

Incorporation of Shoemakers, Linlithgow: records 1658–1913

International PEN, Scottish Centre: further corresp and papers 1953–83

Saltire Society records 1937–85

Scottish Convention of Women records 1974–86

Trinity Bowling Club, Edinburgh: records 1855–1967

Kinross-shire Liberal Association records 1889–1931

MS of 'Regiam Maiestatem' and other Scots laws, late 14th cent

The 'Fowlis Easter Breviary', 15th cent

NATIONAL LIBRARY OF WALES

DEPARTMENT OF MANUSCRIPTS AND RECORDS, ABERYSTWYTH SY23 3BU

Anwyl family of Chester and Pontypridd: corresp and papers 1848–1983

Richard Ithamar Aaron (1901–87), philosopher: papers

Keith Lander Best, MP: Ynys Mon constituency corresp and papers 1979–87

Leonard Eliot Crawshay-Williams (1879–1962), MP and writer: papers

Gareth RV Jones (1905–35), journalist: papers

Thomas Jones, antiquary and genealogist: pedigree roll 1583

Thomas Letts, publisher of Letts diaries: journals of tours in N Wales 1833–34

David Lloyd George, 1st Earl Lloyd-George: further corresp and papers 1890–1939

Thomas Roberts (1816–87), Independent minister: diaries

William Spurrell (1813–89), printer and publisher: papers

Arthur John Williams (c1835–1911) MP: papers

Erbistock, Denbighs: deeds 1413–c1902

Welsh National Opera Ltd: records 1943–83

Western Mail & Echo Ltd, Cardiff: records 1869–1980

Cowethas Flamank (Cornish current affairs and research group): records 1969–83

Wales Tourist Board minutes 1948–70

NATIONAL MARITIME MUSEUM

GREENWICH, LONDON SE10 9NF

Thomas Clifford, 1st Baron Clifford: papers rel to Dutch wars 1652–73

Dobbie family, naval officers: papers, incl those of Captain William Hugh Dobbie 1805–15 and Admiral William Hugh Dobbie 1840–74

Fowke family, naval officers: papers 1745–1908, incl those of Rear-Admiral Thorpe Fowke 1745–59 and Vice-Admiral George Fowke 1781–1819

Vice-Admiral Henry Carr Glyn: corresp and papers 1852–82

Rear-Admiral Sir James Hillyar: papers rel to capture of USS *Essex* 1813–14

Admiral Sir Robert Brice Kingsmill, 1st Bt, MP (addnl): papers c1750–1803

William V Maybury, convict: journal of voyage to Sydney 1828

Furness Withy & Co plc, shipowners, London: further records c1891–1982, incl records of British Maritime Trust Ltd

Shipbuilders and Repairers National Association: further records c1942–77

NOTTINGHAM UNIVERSITY

UNIVERSITY LIBRARY, MANUSCRIPTS DEPARTMENT, UNIVERSITY PARK, NOTTINGHAM NG7 2RD

Bromley family, baronets, of East Stoke: further deeds 1607–1870

Park Pharmacy, Nottingham: prescription books c1920–29

Nottingham Corporation waterworks: minute books 20th cent

OXFORD UNIVERSITY

DEPARTMENT OF WESTERN MANUSCRIPTS, BODLEIAN LIBRARY, OXFORD OX1 3BG

Wilberforce family (addnl): papers 18th–19th cent, incl corresp and diaries of William Wilberforce (1759–1833), MP and philanthropist and corresp of Robert Isaac Wilberforce (1802–1857), archdeacon of the East Riding

Thomas Aldersey, barrister-at-law: theological notebooks 1653–87

Sir Augustus Wall Callcott (1779–1844), painter and Maria, Lady Callcott (1785–1842), author: papers

William Horsley (1774–1858), composer and John Callcott Horsley (1817–1903), painter: papers

Sir Gore Ouseley, 1st Bt, diplomat: diary 1810–15

Sir Edmund John Monson, 1st Bt, diplomat (addnl): corresp 1853–1904

Henry Edward Duke, 1st Baron Merrivale: papers 1916–19

Maurice Francis Headlam (1873–1956), civil servant: papers

Sir Neil Marten (1916–86) MP: papers

RHODES HOUSE LIBRARY, SOUTH PARKS ROAD, OXFORD OX1 3RG

United Society for the Propagation of the Gospel: records 18th–20th cent

Sir Harry Fagg Batterbee (1880–1976), High Commissioner to New Zealand: further papers

Sir Cecil Clementi: papers as governor of Hong Kong 1925–31

Sir Miles Clifford: papers as governor of the Falkland Islands 1946–54 etc

Brigadier David Mercer MacDougall: papers as colonial secretary of Hong Kong 1946–49

PUSEY HOUSE, OXFORD OX1 3LZ

Charles Abel Heurtley (1806–95), professor of divinity: further corresp and autographs collected by his daughter Ellen

Huxley family papers c1840–1950, incl letters of Thomas Arnold and Mrs Humphry Ward

MIDDLE EAST CENTRE, ST ANTONY'S COLLEGE, OXFORD OX2 6JF

Jerusalem and the East Mission: further papers c1910–59

JAM Faraday, Palestine Police: papers rel to Safad and Jaffa disturbances 1929–33

PUBLIC RECORD OFFICE

CHANCERY LANE, LONDON WC2A 1LR

Account roll of the Great Wardrobe *temp* Richard II

Neville family, Barons Braybrooke: further family papers (PRO 30/50)

PUBLIC RECORD OFFICE OF NORTHERN IRELAND

66 BALMORAL AVENUE, BELFAST BT9 6NY

Hill family, baronets, of Brook Hall, co Londonderry: family and estate papers *c*1660–1900, incl papers of Hugh Rowley as storekeeper of the ordnance 1690–92 and corresp and papers of Sir George Fitzgerald Hill (1763–1839) 2nd Bt, MP

Lowry-Corry family, Earls Belmore: further accounts etc 1798–1902

Perceval-Maxwell family of Tallow, co Waterford: estate papers 1775–1969

Sir William James Bull, 1st Bt, MP: letters and papers rel to Ulster gun-running 1913-14

Francis Rawdon Chesney, general and explorer: corresp, journal and papers 1823–85, mainly rel to his Euphrates Valley expedition

Robert Hanna, grocer, Limerick: diary 1856–62

Barrington & Son, solicitors, Dublin and Limerick: clients papers, incl estate papers of the Loftus family, Marquesses of Ely 1637–1928, Robinson family, baronets, of Rokeby, co Louth 1677–1903 and the Maguire family of Tempo, co Fermanagh 1631–1893

Drapers Company of London: estate and legal papers rel to Draperstown and Moneymore, co Londonderry 1585–1933

Blackwood & Jury, architects, Belfast: records 1933–70

R & H Hall Ltd, grain importers, Belfast: accounts 1935–71

WH Kane & Co Ltd, iron founders, Larne: records 1917–79

Londonderry Gaslight Co: records 1829–1987

Central Council for the Organisation of Recruiting in Ireland: corresp etc 1914–20

MV *Princess Victoria*: log and papers rel to the loss of the ship etc 1890–1953

READING UNIVERSITY

UNIVERSITY LIBRARY, WHITEKNIGHTS, READING RG6 2AE

John Payne: account book rel to corn and oil mills in W Yorkshire etc 1802–11

Addington, Kent: tithe book 1843

Heinemann Educational Books Ltd, publishers: corresp 1946–80

Routledge & Kegan Paul Ltd, publishers: further papers 1969–79

INSTITUTE OF AGRICULTURAL HISTORY, WHITEKNIGHTS, READING RG6 2AG

Council for National Parks records *c*1960–80

Council for the Protection of Rural England: further records 1934–81

Farm management survey returns 1936–73; national investigation into the economics of milk production returns 1934–62

ROYAL COLLEGE OF PHYSICIANS OF LONDON

11 ST ANDREWS PLACE, LONDON NW1 4LE

Walter Russell Brain, 1st Baron Brain (1895–1966): corresp and papers

Sir William Henry Broadbent, 1st Bt: papers rel to illnesses of the royal family 1891–92

ROYAL COLLEGE OF SURGEONS OF ENGLAND

35–43 LINCOLN'S INN FIELDS,
LONDON WC2A 3PN

Sir John Charles Nicholson, 3rd Bt: student notes and records of operations 1929–76

ST ANDREWS UNIVERSITY

UNIVERSITY LIBRARY, ST ANDREWS,
FIFE KY16 9TR

John Bethune of Blebo: account book 1720–40

John Cook (1739–1815), professor of moral philosophy: lectures on pneumatics

Arthur Thomson (1907–87), philosopher: corresp and papers

SCIENCE MUSEUM LIBRARY

LONDON SW7 5NH

Archibald Smith, mathematician: note-book on magnetism 1839–47

Cambridge University and Town Gas Light Co records 1903–27

Log book of steam yacht *Anthracite* May–Sept 1880

SCOTTISH RECORD OFFICE

HM GENERAL REGISTER HOUSE,
PRINCES STREET, EDINBURGH EH1 3YY

Balfour family, Earls of Balfour: family papers 19th–20th cent, incl political papers of Arthur James Balfour (1848–1930), 1st Earl and Gerald William Balfour (1853–1945), 2nd Earl

Campbell family of Jura: further family papers 1663–1810

McNeill family of Taynish, Argyllshire: deeds 1402–19th cent

Cringletie estate, Peeblesshire: papers 14th–19th cent

Pentland barony, Midlothian: court book 1678–97

Deans of the Chapel Royal: records 1609–1960

Original Secession Church, Infirmary St, Edinburgh: managers minutes 1802–42 (transferred from National L of Scotland)

Association of Government Land Valuation Assessors of Scotland: minutes 1904–57

Educational Institute of Scotland: further records 1731–1963

Edinburgh Natural History Society: minutes, incl predecessor bodies, 1869–1980

SOCIETY OF FRIENDS

FRIENDS HOUSE, EUSTON ROAD,
LONDON NW1 2BJ

Jane Pontefract: papers rel to relief work in Poland 1921–26

Rachel Wilson of Kendal: letters (26) 1768–69

Association for Promoting the Training of Women Teachers: records 1870–1943

SOUTHAMPTON UNIVERSITY

UNIVERSITY LIBRARY, HIGHFIELD,
SOUTHAMPTON SO9 5NH

Ashley, Cooper, Lamb and Temple families: family papers, incl letter books of Sir William Temple 1647–81, corresp and diaries of Henry Temple (1739–1802), 2nd Viscount Palmerston, family and political corresp and diaries of Henry John Temple (1784–1865), 3rd Viscount Palmerston, papers of William Cowper-Temple (1811–88), Baron Mount Temple and corresp of Anthony Ashley Cooper (1801–85), 7th Earl of Shaftesbury and Wilfrid William Ashley (1867–1938), Baron Mount Temple; Temple family estate papers, England and Ireland (transferred from Hants RO), incl Romsey manor views of frankpledge, presentments and rentals 1607–1846

Richard Colley Wellesley (1760–1842), Marquess Wellesley and Richard Wellesley (1787–1831) MP: personal and family papers c1792–1913

Martin VO Bell, poet: corresp and poems 1939–45

Harry Rothwell (1902–80), historian: papers rel to historical geography of Hampshire

William Wynn Simpson (1907–87), general secretary of the Council of Christians and Jews: papers

Council of Christians and Jews: records 1941–86

STRATHCLYDE UNIVERSITY

UNIVERSITY ARCHIVES, MCCANCE
BUILDING, 16 RICHMOND STREET,
GLASGOW G1 1XQ

Leith-Buchanan family, baronets, of Ross and Drummakil, Dunbartonshire: family and estate papers c1630–1930

TATE GALLERY

TATE GALLERY ARCHIVE, MILLBANK,
LONDON SW1P 4RG

David Garshen Bomberg (1890–1957), painter: corresp and papers

Sir Jacob Epstein, sculptor: letters to his daughter Peggy Jean Lewis 1948–59

Edward FW James, poet and art patron: letters to René Magritte 1937–40

Ben Nicholson (1894–1982), painter: corresp and papers

Sir John KM Rothenstein, director: corresp and papers 1913–87

Madge and Fred Staite-Murray: corresp 1927–72, incl letters from Barbara Hepworth and Ben Nicholson

Alfred Turner (1874–1940), sculptor: corresp

Hanover Gallery, London: records rel to Francis Bacon 1944–62

VICTORIA AND ALBERT MUSEUM

NATIONAL ART LIBRARY, VICTORIA AND
ALBERT MUSEUM, LONDON SW7 2RL

Reginald Hallward, artist: letters from Louis David 1902–13

Cyrus Hill, glass designer: recipe book c1840–60

Richard Redgrave, landscape and genre painter: family letters 1836–89

Francis Tuckett: travel diary, Stockholm to Aachen, 1824

Derry Ormond House, Bettws Bledrws, Cardiganshire: inventories 1868–1944

ARCHIVE OF ART AND DESIGN,
23 BLYTHE ROAD, LONDON W14 0QF

Edith and Nelson Dawson, silversmiths: records c1890–1930

W Gordon Hunton (1885–1933), textile designer: business records and designs

Francis Marshall (*d*1980), illustrator and writer: sketch books and papers

The Ambassador magazine: records *c*1935–70

William Comyns & Sons Ltd, manufacturing silversmiths, London: records *c*1900–86

UNIVERSITY OF WALES

DEPARTMENT OF MANUSCRIPTS, THE LIBRARY, UNIVERSITY COLLEGE OF NORTH WALES, BANGOR LL57 2DG

Robert Silyn Roberts, social reformer: further letters and papers *c*1904–30

Workers Educational Association, North Wales district: records 1925–73

WARWICK UNIVERSITY

MODERN RECORDS CENTRE, UNIVERSITY OF WARWICK LIBRARY, COVENTRY CV4 7AL

William Henry Stokes (1894–1977), trade union official: further papers

Rover Co Ltd, motor car mfrs, Solihull: records 1890–1972

Engineering Employers Federation: further records of Coventry 1909–64, Derby 1923–69, Leicester 1872–1968, Lincoln 1947–72 and Nottingham 1918–40 district associations

Central Council of Bank Staff Associations records 1923–63

Grimsby Steam and Diesel Fishing Vessels Engineers and Firemens Union: minutes 1900–87

National Amalgamated Union of Life Assurance Workers: further records, incl National Union of Co-operative Insurance Agents

National Graphical Association: further records 1872–1985

National Society of Metal Mechanics records 1873–1979

Society of Telecommunication Engineers, London branch: records 1946–74

WELLCOME INSTITUTE FOR THE HISTORY OF MEDICINE

183 EUSTON ROAD, LONDON NW1 2BP

Western MSS Collection

Liston family: papers, incl letters (275) from Robert Liston, surgeon, to James Miller 1834–45

John Fairbank, dental surgeon, London: ledger 1883

Thomas Graham, naval surgeon: diary of passage to China 1849–50

General Apothecaries Co Ltd, chemists and druggists, London: records 1855–1951

Contemporary Medical Archives Centre

Robina Addis (1900–86), psychiatric social worker: corresp and papers

Alfred Glucksman (1904–85), medical scientist: corresp and papers

Donald Hunter (1898–1979), physician: misc papers

Robert Gwyn Macfarlane (1907–86), pathologist: papers, incl working papers for his biographies of Sir Alexander Fleming and Lord Florey

Milos Sekulich (1900–86), physician: corresp and papers

Constance Wood (1897–1985), radiologist: corresp and papers

Child Accident Prevention Trust records 1979–87

Medical Research Council Cyclotron Unit records *c*1934–60, incl minutes of Radium Beam Therapy Research Committee 1934–39

National Birthday Trust Fund records 1929–87

YORK MINSTER LIBRARY

DEAN'S PARK, YORK YO1 2JD

General John Hodgson: letter book
1805–06

Convocation of the province of York
minutes 1931–61

Purey-Cust Nursing Home records
1880–1984

Girls Friendly Society, York diocesan
council: minutes 1881–1971

Yorkshire Philosophical Society records
20th cent

YORK UNIVERSITY

BORTHWICK INSTITUTE OF HISTORICAL
RESEARCH, ST ANTHONY'S HALL,
YORK YO1 2PW

Keesberry Hall manor, Cawood: court
rolls 1789–1936

Rural Deanery records for Ainsty and
Bulmer 19th–20th cent

Catholic Apostolic Church: records of
Yorkshire churches 1867–1959

Church of England Mens Society, York
diocesan union: records 20th cent

Community of the Resurrection,
Mirfield: further records 20th cent

Local Repositories: England

AVON

BATH CITY RECORD OFFICE, GUILDHALL,
BATH BA1 5AW

WT Chesterman & Sons, solicitors:
records 1886–1961

Shutter & Co, paint and wallpaper
merchants: records 1878–1953

Stone, King & Wardle, solicitors: records
1835–1952, deeds and clients papers
1594–1940

Royal United Hospital records
1826–1979

BRISTOL RECORD OFFICE, COUNCIL
HOUSE, COLLEGE GREEN, BRISTOL BS1 5TR

Day family, West India merchants:
account books 1698–1753

Christopher James Thomas of Llanga-
dock, Carms: diary 1828 and misc family
papers c1822–1948

Henbury hundred survey c1810

TW Baker & Son, motor body builders,
Bedminster: day book 1920–33

F Braby & Co Ltd, zinc and galvanised
iron mfrs, Bristol and Deptford: records
c1850–1962

Central Electricity Generating Board,
Fossil Fuel Supplies Division C: records
c1948–65

Edward Thrissell, rope mfr: inventories
and accounts 1787

Bristol Guild of the Handicapped records
1897–1986

British Association for the Advancement
of Science, Bristol meeting: minutes
1896–98

Electrical Association for Women:
minutes of Bristol, Thornbury and
Weston-super-Mare branches 1968–86

BEDFORDSHIRE

BEDFORDSHIRE RECORD OFFICE, COUNTY
HALL, BEDFORD MK42 9AP

Brooks family of Flitwick: further diaries
1840–59 and MS of JT Brooks 'Hortus
Botanicus Flitwickiensis' c1838–42

VH Chambers, naturalist, Meppershall: papers 1922–75

George Glazier, county librarian: papers c1920–59

William and Joseph Barber of Stopsley, Luton: farm account books 1815–37

Kingswood, chemists, Potton: prescription books 1924–76

Luton Water Co records 1865–1972

Simplex Mechanical Handling Co Ltd, Bedford: records 1911–79

Turvey Congregational Church records 1829–1987

Bakewell Snugs drinking club, Derbys: records 1809–23

BERKSHIRE

BERKSHIRE RECORD OFFICE, SHIRE HALL, SHINFIELD PARK, READING RG2 9XD

John Egham Little of Uffington, local historian: working papers 20th cent

Sigmund Pulsometer Pumps Ltd, pump mfrs, Reading: records 20th cent

Newbury Rural Deanery and Newbury Clerical Club records 19th–20th cent

Reading Labour Party records 20th cent

Slough Conservative Association records 1953–78

BUCKINGHAMSHIRE

BUCKINGHAMSHIRE RECORD OFFICE, COUNTY HALL, AYLESBURY HP20 1UA

Barrington family, Viscounts Barrington: Westbury deeds 16th cent–1854

Browne family of Aylesbury and Maids Moreton: corresp and papers, incl papers of Sir Thomas Gore Browne at Corfu 1833–34

Collet family of the Hale, Wendover (addnl): account roll rel to the estate of John Colet, dean of St Paul's, 1514–15

Webster & Cannon Ltd, builders and contractors, Aylesbury: records 1885–1946

Royal Bucks Hussars records 1915–65

Wooburn parish census 1801

Transferred from Buckinghamshire Archaeological Society:

Buckinghamshire manor court rolls and records 14th cent–c1930

CAMBRIDGESHIRE

CAMBRIDGESHIRE RECORD OFFICE, SHIRE HALL, CAMBRIDGE CB3 0AP

Hall family of Weston Colville (addnl): estate papers 1820–1900

Coveney tithe apportionment 1846

Barcham Farm, Soham: records 1915–56

Metcalfe, Copeman & Pettefar, solicitors, Wisbech (addnl): family and business records 1741–1919

Bacon Bros, tobacconists, Cambridge: records 1831–1980

Hockey & Son, estate agents, Cambridge: records 1925–70

Douglas L January & Partners, estate agents, Cambridge: records 1937–87

JO Vinter & Son Ltd, coal merchants, Cambridge: further records 1883–1967

JP Young, draper, Cambridge: ledger 1905–11

National Union of Teachers, South Cambridgeshire branch: records 1935–86

Grunty Fen Drainage Commissioners records 1861–1971

Littleport and Downham District Internal Drainage Board: further records 1756–1976

Caldecote, Long Stanton and Babraham, Cambs, and Hargham, Norfolk, etc deeds early 13th cent–1346

CAMBRIDGESHIRE RECORD OFFICE,
GRAMMAR SCHOOL WALK,
HUNTINGDON PE18 6LF

Fellowes family, Barons de Ramsey: further estate papers 17th cent–1952

Sismey family of Offord Cluny: further papers

Charles Frederick Tebbut, local historian (addnl): working papers 1940–62

Inclosure awards for Great Catworth 1799, Everton 1804, Stow Longa 1841 and Yelling 1822

Beachampstead in Great Staughton manor records 17th cent – 1925

Maps of the manors of Gaines in Great Staughton, Perry and Midloe 1801

John Edwards, butcher, St Ives: ledger 1833–43

Everton with Tetworth parish records 1628–1866 (transferred from Bedfordshire RO)

St Ives parish records 1561–1981

Catworth Town Land Charity records 1871–1969

Duke of Manchester's Light Horse records 1859–82

CHESHIRE

CHESHIRE RECORD OFFICE, DUKE STREET,
CHESTER CH1 1RL

Robert Davies & Co, solicitors, Warrington: deeds and clients papers 14th–20th cent

CHESTER CITY RECORD OFFICE,
TOWN HALL, CHESTER CH1 2HJ

Thomas Harrison (1744–1829), architect: further drawings

Smiths, Cutlers and Plumbers Company records 1637–1983

WARRINGTON LIBRARY,
MUSEUM STREET, WARRINGTON WA1 1JB

Thomas Wright of Marbury House Farm: papers 1824–1913

Holes Lane Farm, Woolston: deeds 1733–1883

CLEVELAND

CLEVELAND COUNTY ARCHIVES
DEPARTMENT, EXCHANGE HOUSE,
6 MARTON ROAD,
MIDDLESBROUGH TS1 1DB

Guisborough Provident Industrial Co-operative Society Ltd: records 1874–1975

Cleveland, Durham and North Yorkshire Institute for the Blind: records 1898–1975

Sir William Turner's Hospital, Kirkleatham: records 1676–1952 (transferred from N Yorks RO)

Guisborough Liberal Association minutes 1889–1950

CORNWALL

CORNWALL RECORD OFFICE,
COUNTY HALL, TRURO TR1 3AY

Bickle family: engineering papers 19th cent

Scoble family: letters from Nevada and Mexico c1870–79

Williams family of Werrington Park, Devon and Caerhays Castle: estate papers 15th–19th cent

Matthew Paul Moyle, meteorologist and surgeon: family corresp 1835–50

Parnall, Finn, Langford & Busby, solicitors, Launceston: deeds and papers 18th–20th cent

St Erney parish records from 1555

Falmouth Baptist Church: further records 1812–58

Coinagehall Street Wesleyan Methodist Church, Helston: further records from 1834

Mawgan in Meneage Wesleyan Methodist records from 1835

Penzance Wesleyan Methodist Circuit records from 1800

Truro Wesleyan Methodist Circuit (addnl): preachers minutes from 1819

Federation of Catholic Priests, Truro Diocesan Association and Ward: minutes 1917–30

Girls Friendly Society, Penzance and Lands End branches: records c1870–1939

CUMBRIA

CUMBRIA RECORD OFFICE, THE CASTLE, CARLISLE CA3 8UR

MacInnes family of Rickerby House, Carlisle (addnl): Cumberland, London and Middlesex estate papers 18th–20th cent

Muckle, Son & Hall, solicitors, Alston: business and clients papers c1660–20th cent

Cowans, Sheldon & Co Ltd, crane mfrs, Carlisle (addnl): records 19th–20th cent

Silloth Motor & Engineering Co Ltd: records 1929–77

Whitehaven & West Cumberland Auctioneering Co Ltd: records 1873–20th cent

Fisher Street United Reformed Church, Carlisle: records 1742–1981

CUMBRIA RECORD OFFICE, 140 DUKE STREET, BARROW-IN-FURNESS LA14 1XW

Petty and Postlethwaite families, bankers, of Bardsea and Ulverston: family, business and estate papers 16th–20th cent

John Case of Little Urswick: waste book 1800

CUMBRIA RECORD OFFICE, COUNTY OFFICES, KENDAL LA9 4RQ

Parkin family of Howtown: corresp, deeds and papers 18th–20th cent

Rigg family of Crossrigg Hall: deeds and papers 1748–1911

Salkeld family of Temple Sowerby: corresp c1840–75

Gatey, Heelis & Co, solicitors, Hawkshead: further clients papers 17th–18th cent

Miller & Co, solicitors, Cambridge: deeds and papers of Foxghyll, Loughrigg 1818–1900 (transferred from Cambs RO)

Thomas Bakeson and Joseph Severs, chemists, Kendal: financial records 1872–1901

Raymond Jay, architect, Hawkshead: records 1955–85

James Longstaff, builder and joiner, Warcop: accounts 1845–1920

Middleton (Kendal) Ltd, ironmongers (addnl): records 1914–38

Provincial Insurance Co Ltd, Kendal: further records c1900–70

Woolleys, drapers, Kendal: records 1928–61

Shearmen's Company, Kendal: book of records 1579–1777

National Union of Teachers, South Westmorland district minutes 1911–81

DERBYSHIRE

DERBYSHIRE RECORD OFFICE,
COUNTY OFFICES, MATLOCK DE4 3AG

Wilmot-Horton family, baronets, of Osmaston: family and estate papers 13th–20th cent, incl political and administrative papers of Sir Robert Wilmot (*d*1772), 1st Bt and Sir Robert John Wilmot-Horton (1784-1841), 3rd Bt (transferred from Derby Central L)

Bagshaw, Bateman and White families: deeds and family papers 17th–20th cent

Ward and Jenkinson families of Cowley, Dronfield and Unstone: deeds and family corresp 1773–1956, incl account book of Thomas Jenkinson, hatter 1836–47

Repton inclosure award 1769

Jones & Middleton, solicitors, Chesterfield: Eyam deeds 1756–1958, Chesterfield deeds 1632–1914 and clients papers mid 19th–20th cent

Barnes family, tailors, Belper: accounts 1851–88

Joseph Bourne & Son Ltd, pottery mfrs, Denby: records, incl Bourne family papers *c*1806–1979

James Foster, baker and grocer, Derby: accounts and personal papers 1866–1929

Harry Shreeve, grocer, Darley Abbey: accounts and personal papers 1882–1916

St Mary's parish, Ilkeston: records 1588–1985

Osmaston Road Baptist Church, Derby: records 1832–1981

Parwich United Charities records 1778–1944

Nottinghamshire Miners Association, South Normanton branch: records 1919–45

DEVON

DEVON RECORD OFFICE, CASTLE STREET,
EXETER EX4 3PU

Templer family of Lindridge (addnl): misc papers 18th–19th cent

CR Claridge & Sons Ltd, timber merchants and motor vehicle dealers, Exeter and Heythrop, Oxon: records 1895–1973

Samuel Forward, attorney, Axminster: day book 1785–95

Southern National Omnibus Co Ltd records 1929–82

West of England Fire & Life Insurance Co, Exmouth agent: policy ledgers 1808–21, 1868–89

Dartmouth Baptist Church records 1786–1980

Teignbridge District Council: S Devon sea fishery records 1855–1939

WEST DEVON RECORD OFFICE, UNIT 3,
CLARE PLACE, COXSIDE,
PLYMOUTH PL4 0JW

Culme-Seymour family, baronets, of Rockingham Castle, Northants: papers *c*1877–1960

Caroline Treby of Goodamoor: diaries 1803–31

Charles Harding (Plymouth) Ltd, house furnishers: day books 1910–45

JF Hussell, ironmongers and builders merchants, Plymouth: records 1882–1982

RJ Mitchell & Son (Plymouth) Ltd, wholesale corn merchants: business records 1912–74 and family papers 19th–20th cent

Anthony charity, Yealmpton: records 1856–1941

DORSET

DORSET RECORD OFFICE, COUNTY HALL, DORCHESTER DT1 1XJ

Langton Herring estate: further papers 1786–1918

Haydon Common inclosure award and map 1886

Maiden Newton tithe map 1838; Stock Gaylard tithe map and apportionment 1841

Blake, Lapthorn, solicitors, Portsmouth: deeds and clients papers 17th–19th cent, incl Kiddle and Jones family papers 1773–1892

Collissons, solicitors, London (addnl): deeds and clients papers 1763–1930, incl Parnham estate

Dibbens, solicitors, Wimborne: Blandford Forum deeds 1727–1948

Lock, Reed & Lock, solicitors, Dorchester (addnl): probate papers 1727–1898

Lott & Walne Ltd, engineers and iron founders, Fordington: records 1932–48

Staniland, architects, Bournemouth: plans and drawings 19th–20th cent

Wimborne Minster (addnl): deanery account roll 1507–08

Rural Deanery records for Bere Regis 1859–1972, Blandford 1856–86, Milton and Blandford c1886–1977

Parish records of Tarrant Crawford 1597–1940 and further records of Wimborne St Giles 1589–1685

Sherborne Methodist Circuit (addnl): records 1818–1981

Bournemouth and Christchurch Board of Guardians records 1728–1948

DURHAM

COUNTY RECORD OFFICE, COUNTY HALL, DURHAM DH1 5UL

Fowler family, grocers, Durham: papers c1750–1950

Peele and Sadler families of Durham: papers c1895–1960

Vane-Tempest-Stewart family, Marquesses of Londonderry: further estate papers 19th–20th cent

William Neal Davis: papers 1920–57

Sir Cuthbert Morley Headlam (1876–1964) Bt, MP: further papers

Charles Wilson of Willington: papers 1891–1968

Watsons, solicitors, Barnard Castle: further records 19th–20th cent

Thornley Colliery records 19th–20th cent

Cornsay common and almshouses: papers rel to c1730–1959

ESSEX

ESSEX RECORD OFFICE, COUNTY HALL, CHELMSFORD CM1 1LX

Frances Evelyn (Daisy) Greville, Countess of Warwick: letters to Sir Joseph Laycock 1902

Barringtons manor court rolls and extent 1602–95; Corringham manor records 1631–1935; Crouchmans manor court roll 1682; Hatfield Peverel manor court books 1645–1929; Uphall manor deeds and papers 1631–1803

Chelmer & Blackwater Navigation Co: further records 1716–1977

SG Swayne Ltd, production engineers, Romford: records 1916–80

London Road Congregational Church, Chelmsford: further accounts 1792–1848

Age Concern, Essex: records 1957–82

Felsted charities (addnl): accounts and school records 1877–1938

National Farmers Union, Essex branch records 1921–76

Woodford United Military Brass Band: further records 1892–1946

ESSEX RECORD OFFICE, COLCHESTER AND
NORTH-EAST ESSEX BRANCH,
STANWELL HOUSE, STANWELL STREET,
COLCHESTER CO2 7DL

William Byfield, apothecary, Colchester (addnl): diary and papers 1834–59

Records of Colchester charities of Finch 1685–1835, Winnock 1689–1924 and Winsley 1734–1971

ESSEX RECORD OFFICE, SOUTHEND
BRANCH, CENTRAL LIBRARY,
VICTORIA AVENUE,
SOUTHEND-ON-SEA SS2 6EX

Canewdon Hall manor stewards papers 1814–53

James Kerr, Son & Co, tailors, Southend: ledgers 1915–80

Great Stambridge parish records 1559–1903

GLOUCESTERSHIRE

GLOUCESTERSHIRE RECORD OFFICE,
CLARENCE ROW, OFF ALVIN STREET,
GLOUCESTER GL1 3DW

Eley and Marling families of Berkeley, Stroud and Thornbury: papers 19th–20th cent

Charles Bannister, botanist, Ashchurch: ornithological journals and botanical papers 1936–80

Newent manor estreats 1430–31

Haines & Sumner, solicitors, Gloucester: further clients papers 19th–20th cent

Ticehurst, Wyatt & Co, solicitors, Cheltenham (addnl): estate papers 17th–20th cent; Cheltenham manor records 19th–20th cent; letter books c1812–65

Brices Farm, Westerleigh: labour account 1884–1934

Dyke House fruit farm, Bromsberrow: accounts 1928–68

Cavendish House (Cheltenham) Ltd, drapers: deeds 1823–1947

Field family, carpenters, Arlington and Winson: records 1871–1958

John Gardner, brewer, Cheltenham: accounts 1800–14

Gloucester Bell Hotel Co Ltd (addnl): minutes 1864–97

WJB Halls Ltd, builders and joinery mfrs, Gloucester: accounts c1917–45

Healing & Overbury, architects and surveyors, Cheltenham: papers rel to buildings in Gloucestershire and Worcestershire c1905–45

Waller Son & Wood, architects and surveyors, Gloucester (addnl): records c1860–1940

Tewkesbury Congregational Church records 1819–1977

English Folk Dance and Song Society, Gloucester district branch: records c1936–80

Stroud and district Nursing Association records 1893–1965

Hewelsfield police station diary 1840–43

HAMPSHIRE

HAMPSHIRE RECORD OFFICE,
20 SOUTHGATE STREET,
WINCHESTER SO23 9EF

Gunner family, farmers and hop growers, Alton: papers from 1844

Hillier family, nurserymen: further papers 1844–20th cent

Sherwood family: papers 1583–19th cent

Stephen Gardiner, bishop of Winchester: household account book 1547–51

Sumner Wilson, vicar of Preston Candover: papers from 1803

Isington deeds 13th–17th cent

George James Bassett, ironmonger, Petersfield: personal and business papers 20th cent

J Payne & Son, builders and decorators, Lyndhurst: records from 1951

Rose & Alexander, ironmongers, Fordingbridge: records from 1851

Andover Baptist Church records 1825–20th cent

Manchester Unity of Oddfellows, Loyal Philanthropic Lodge, Alton: records from 1845

Binstead Home Guard records c1940–45

PORTSMOUTH CITY RECORDS OFFICE, 3 MUSEUM ROAD, PORTSMOUTH PO1 2LE

Hoad & Sons, vehicle builders: records 1777–1980

Portsea Island Mutual Co-operative Society Ltd: records 20th cent

SOUTHAMPTON CITY RECORD OFFICE, CIVIC CENTRE, SOUTHAMPTON SO9 4XR

Chalcroft Farm, Westend: records 1822–1943, incl Owton family papers

Moodys, boat builders: day book 1735–52

Southampton Free Church Federal Council records 1930–69

HEREFORD AND WORCESTER

HEREFORD AND WORCESTER RECORD OFFICE, COUNTY HALL, SPETCHLEY ROAD, WORCESTER WR5 2NP

Norgrove Court, Redditch: deeds 15th–19th cent

Beckford manor records c1455–1858

St Helen's, Worcester churchwardens accounts c1519–20

Worcester Co-operative Party records 1950–82

Severn-Trent Water Authority: further records 1881–1975

HEREFORD RECORD OFFICE, THE OLD BARRACKS, HAROLD STREET, HEREFORD HR1 2QX

Hazlehurst estate, Walford: deeds c1780–1950

Longlands Bar estate, Dilwyn: deeds 1659–1855

Shobdon estate: corn rent accounts 1857–82

Leominster Toc H records 1938–67

Welsh Water Authority: records 19th–20th cent

HERTFORDSHIRE

HERTFORDSHIRE RECORD OFFICE, COUNTY HALL, HERTFORD SG13 8DE

Ware Charity estates: further deeds 1377–1702

Hormead Redeswell manor court books 1712–67

Temple Dinsley manor: further records 1491–1741

Samuel Andrews, builder, Hertford: records 1806–16

George Lines & Co, chemists, Hertford: prescription books 1841–1987

Ardley parish records 1546–1987

Green Coat School, Hertford: records 1764–1895

Amalgamated Society of Woodworkers, Hertford branch: records 1894–1953

Hertford Book Society minutes 1815–59

Hertford Corps Dramatique records 1852–76

National Playing Fields Association, Hertfordshire branch: minutes 1926–59

Labour Party branch records for Hatfield 1947–66, Potters Bar 1955–81

Queens Regiment of Dragoon Guards: sergeant-major's orderly books 1798–99

HUMBERSIDE

CITY RECORD OFFICE, 79 LOWGATE, KINGSTON UPON HULL HU1 2AA

Premier Oil Extracting Mills Ltd: records 20th cent

Waterloo Mills Cake & Warehousing Co Ltd, seed crushers and animal feedstuffs mfrs: records 1879–1968

KENT

KENT ARCHIVES OFFICE, COUNTY HALL, MAIDSTONE ME14 1XQ

Gathorne-Hardy family, Earls of Cranbrook: corresp 1759–1902

Bredgar parish: further records 1546–1926

King Charles the Martyr Church, Tunbridge Wells: records 1709–1984

Old Meeting House (Unitarian), Tenterden: records 1744–1854

Tonbridge Methodist Circuit records 1838–1981

Malling Place private mental hospital, West Malling: records 1829–1977

Canterbury Citizens Advice Bureau records 1941–84

KENT ARCHIVES OFFICE, SOUTH EAST KENT AREA, CENTRAL LIBRARY, GRACE HILL, FOLKESTONE CT20 1HD

Gertrude Ashworth of St Margarets Bay: diaries 1898–1986

CP Davies, librarian and local historian: papers c1885–1985

National Union of Mineworkers, Kent area: records c1915–80

KENT ARCHIVES OFFICE, NORTH EAST KENT AREA, RAMSGATE LIBRARY, GUILDFORD LAWN, RAMSGATE CT11 9AI

Kennett Beacham Martin, deputy harbour-master, Ramsgate: MS history of the Royal Harbour 1831

LANCASHIRE

LANCASHIRE RECORD OFFICE, BOW LANE, PRESTON PR1 8ND

Blundell family of Crosby: further family and estate papers 14th cent – c1970

Walmesley family of Westwood: further family papers 19th–20th cent

Hilda Baker, comedienne: corresp and papers 1943–75

Sir John Gilbert Laithwaite, Indian administrator: corresp and working papers c1940–70

SS Stott Ltd, iron and brass founders, Rossendale: records 1885–1970

Marsden monthly meeting, Society of Friends: further records 19th–20th cent

National Farmers Union, Lancashire county branch: records 1905–85

Lancashire Footwear Manufacturers Association: further records c1970–87

Lancashire Veterinary Association
records 1866–1963

Manchester Unity Independent Order of
Oddfellows, Loyal West Coast Lodge:
records 1866–1967

LEICESTERSHIRE

LEICESTERSHIRE RECORD OFFICE,
57 NEW WALK, LEICESTER LE1 7JB

Cave family, Barons Braye: further
family and estate papers 13th–18th cent

Charnell family of Snareston: family and
estate papers c1180–1782, incl court rolls
of Measham and Twycross manors c1613

Kirkland family of Ashby-de-la-Zouche,
surgeons and physicians: diary
1789–1931

Noel family, Earls of Gainsborough:
further family and estate papers
15th–20th cent

Freer, Bouskell & Co, solicitors,
Leicester: estate papers of the Dixie
family, baronets, of Market Bosworth,
Hazlerigg family, Barons Hazlerigg and
Martin family of Anstey

Manchester Unity Independent Order of
Oddfellows, Loyal Earl Howe Lodge:
records 1837–1979

Market Harborough Oddfellows
Society records 1842–1946

Loughborough Constituency Labour
Party (addnl): records c1930–87

Market Harborough parish census 1811

LINCOLNSHIRE

LINCOLNSHIRE ARCHIVES OFFICE,
THE CASTLE, LINCOLN LN1 3AB

Sanderson and Wells-Cole families:
accounts 1660–1866, incl inventory of
Robert Sanderson, bishop of Lincoln,
1663

Edward Lee Hicks, bishop of Lincoln:
diaries 1910–19

Millicent Hill: diaries 1889–1952

William Paddison, farmer and coal
merchant, Saltfleetby St Peter: corresp
and papers 19th–20th cent

Louth manor court rolls 14th–17th cent

Drewery & Wheeldon, auctioneers,
Gainsborough: records 20th cent

Richardsons, land agents, Stamford:
records 1832–20th cent

Frampton United Charities: deeds and
papers 1589–1889

GREATER LONDON

GREATER LONDON RECORD OFFICE,
40 NORTHAMPTON ROAD,
LONDON EC1R 0HB

Priory estate, Hornsey: records
17th–20th cent

Dunsford manor, Surrey: records, incl
court books 1870–1874

Arcade Property Co Ltd: records
1934–80

Montagu, Loebl, Stanley & Co, stockbrokers, Finsbury: records, incl minutes
1938–86

Smith Kendon Ltd, manufacturing
chemists and confectioners, Southwark:
further records 1827–1978

Toynbee Hall: further records 1887–1986

Brooks's Club records 18th–20th cent,
incl records of St James' Club

Middlesex County Association and
London Diocesan Guild of Church Bell
Ringers: records 1889–1984

National United Temperance Council
records 1897–1982

Royal Choral Society records 19th–20th
cent

Surrey Tabernacle Benefit Society
records c1866–1976

London Labour Party records, incl
minutes 1919–64

Banstead Hospital, Surrey (addnl):
patients records 19th–20th cent

Sir Stuart Sankey (1854–1940), City
Remembrancer: scrap books

King George VI National Memorial
Fund and King George VI Foundation:
records 1952–60

Pepys family: collected papers 1642–99,
incl papers rel to Samuel Pepys

John Pridden, antiquary: topographical
papers rel to St Paul's Cathedral
c1779–1854

William Brass trust: estate papers
1868–1955

Camp Bird Ltd, mining company:
records 1900–63

Exchange Telegraph Co Ltd: records
1872–1969

Farebrother, Ellis & Co, chartered
surveyors: records 1711–1946

Ottoman Bank records 19th–20th cent

Stringer & Richardson, merchants: letter
book 1827–29

Accident Offices Committee: records
1906–78

British Insurance Association: records
1917–70

Fire Offices Committee: records
1861–1985

Grain and Feed Trade Association:
records, incl those of predecessor and
related associations, 1884–1972

Imperial Continental Gas Association
records 1826–1945

National Pawnbrokers Association
records, incl those of predecessor bodies,
1801–1972

Union Society of London: records
1844–1962

Christ's Hospital: further records
15th–20th cent

Belvedere estate, Erith (addnl): corresp
1867–82

Blendon Hall estate, Bexley: papers
1765–1893

William Foster's School, East Wickham:
records 1727–59

Marla Ltd, ladies outfitters, Hackney:
records c1927–77

James Recknell & Co, undertakers,
Dalston: records 1886–1972

Israel Renson, chemist and local
historian, Hackney: papers c1920–86

County of London Volunteer Regt,
1/9 Bn (Stoke Newington): records
1912–20

Sir Oswald Stoll Foundation, Fulham:
records 20th cent

KENSINGTON AND CHELSEA LIBRARIES
AND ARTS SERVICE, CENTRAL LIBRARY,
PHILLIMORE WALK, LONDON W8 7RX

Cowards, chemists, London:
prescription books 1875–1957

LAMBETH ARCHIVES DEPARTMENT,
MINET LIBRARY, 52 KNATCHBULL ROAD,
LONDON SE5 9QY

Minet estate (addnl): Surrey and
Middlesex records 18th–20th cent

SOUTHWARK LOCAL STUDIES LIBRARY,
211 BOROUGH HIGH STREET,
LONDON SE1 1JA

Henry Cox Mason, rector of
Bermondsey: preaching diary 1793–1802

TOWER HAMLETS LOCAL HISTORY
LIBRARY AND ARCHIVES,
227 BANCROFT ROAD, LONDON E1 4DQ

Robert Womersley, industrial chemist,
Spitalfields: account book 1803–63

Oxford House Settlement, Bethnal
Green: records 1886–1986

Bethnal Green Labour Party records
1920–35

WALTHAM FOREST ARCHIVES, VESTRY
HOUSE MUSEUM, VESTRY ROAD,
WALTHAMSTOW, LONDON E17 9NH

Holland family corresp 1844–68

F Clayton (Walthamstow) Ltd, builders:
records 1930–50

Marsh Street and Trinity Congregational
Church, Walthamstow: records
1786–1965

Workers Educational Association,
Leyton branch: records 1944–49

WESTMINSTER CITY LIBRARIES,
LOCAL HISTORY LIBRARY,
MARYLEBONE LIBRARY,
MARYLEBONE ROAD, LONDON NW1 5PS

PC Henry Bendall, Paddington:
notebook 1886–90

GREATER MANCHESTER

GREATER MANCHESTER COUNTY RECORD
OFFICE, 56 MARSHALL STREET,
NEW CROSS, MANCHESTER M4 5FU

Fielden, Harper and Royle families:
Flixton deeds 1627–1950

Davenport family, ropemakers, of
Withington: family and business corresp
and papers c1801–52

H Evers & Co Ltd, road haulage
contractors, Manchester: minute book
1931–67

J Pickup & Sons Ltd, metal bellows mfrs,
Marple: records 1939–75

Reliance Machine Co Ltd, hardware
factors, Manchester: records 20th cent

Trafford Park Cold Storage Ltd,
Manchester: records 1918–70

Dickens Fellowship, Manchester branch:
records c1952–78

Electrical Association for Women,
Urmston and district branch: minutes
1964–75

North West Water Authority records
20th cent

BOLTON ARCHIVE SERVICE, CENTRAL
LIBRARY, CIVIC CENTRE,
LE MANS CRESCENT, BOLTON BL1 1SE

Kay family of Westhoughton and
Mendoza, Argentina: corresp and misc
papers 1870–1923

George Edward Cooper: travel diaries rel
to Italy and Egypt 1884–91

Alice Foley, magistrate: papers rel to local history and the labour movement c1900–73

William Wadsworth & Sons Ltd, lift mfrs: records 1896–1980

Claremont Baptist Church records c1820–1987

Harwood Temperance Sick and Burial Society records 1836–1948

Clement Hughes & Co, solicitors, Prestatyn: Holt and Porter family deeds 18th–19th cent

Bury and Heywood Methodist Circuit records 1795–1980

Stand Grammar School records 1836–1971

Electrical Association for Women, Eccles and district branch: minutes 1938–80

Manchester Regiment records 1758–1960 (transferred from Manchester Central L)

Markland family (addnl): family papers c1700–1821

J Monk Foster (1857–1930), author and local historian (addnl): papers

Gullick Ltd, mining engineers, Wigan: order books 1921–34

Tyldesley and District Industrial Co-operative Society Ltd: records 1904–52

Matthew Lygoe's charity: records 1756–1811

Wigan Bluecoat School records 1862–1982

MERSEYSIDE

Captain James Goffey: papers rel to trade with W Africa c1830–55

William Crawford & Sons Ltd, biscuit mfrs, Liverpool: records c1870–1981, Crawford family papers c1847–1982 and records of 59th Battery, 4th West Lancashire Medium Regt, Royal Artillery

BICC plc, electrical cable mfrs, Prescot: records 19th–20th cent, incl predecessor and subsidiary companies

Dock Labour Joint Committee: further minutes 1962–77

Employers Association of the Port of Liverpool: further minutes 1959–77

Percy Fullerton Corkhill, solicitor and author (addnl): corresp and misc papers 1918–1938

William Nicholson (c1774–1832) of Liverpool: personal and family papers 17th–19th cent

William Rathbone MP, philanthropist: personal and family corresp and misc papers 1855–1930, incl letters (44) from Florence Nightingale 1864–1900

Liverpool Corporation estate rental and survey 1740

Speke Hall estate: further deeds
19th–20th cent

National Association for the Welfare of
Children in Hospital, Liverpool branch:
records 1974–86

Womens International League for Peace
and Freedom, Liverpool branch: records
1942–85

Birkenhead and District Co-operative
Society Ltd: records 1898–1983

HJ Boughey & Son, estate agents,
Wallasey: records c1931–69

GC Milnes, Voss & Co, tramway and
railway carriage builders, Birkenhead:
records 1862–1914, incl records of
George Starbuck & Co 1862–86 and
George F Milnes & Co 1886–1904

Woodfield Cooke, pharmacists, Meols
and Birkenhead: prescription books
c1894–1945

Shaftesbury Boys Club, Birkenhead:
records 1885–1985 (transferred from
Merseyside RO)

WEST MIDLANDS

Berry family: papers rel to air raid
precautions etc 1939–45

George Scott & Sons, wheelwrights and
smiths, Erdington: day book 1889–95

Taylor & Challen Ltd, power press mfrs:
records 1853–1985

Birmingham Wesleyan Methodist
Circuit records 1793–1835; Belmont
Row, Bradford Street, Cherry Street,
Constitution Hill chapels and Islington
Church records 18th–20th cent

Bailey family papers 18th–20th cent

Atkins & Turton, grocers: records 20th
cent

Blackham & Son Ltd, opticians: records
1934–82

Blakemores (Coventry) Ltd, sheet metal
mfrs: records 1893–1985

Bretts Stamping Co Ltd, metal stampers:
order book 20th cent

Coventry Motor Fittings Co Ltd, motor
accessory mfrs: records 1915–81

Warwick Road United Reformed
Church records 18th–20th cent

Trustees of the General Municipal
Charities: records 18th–20th cent

Bablake School: records 18th–20th cent,
incl Fairfax Charity School 1751–1888

Electrical Association for Women,
Coventry branch: minutes 1935–81

National Society of Metal Mechanics,
Coventry branch: contributions books
1896–1986

National Union of Vehicle Builders,
Coventry branch: records 1855–66,
1909–72

Coventry Friendly and Provident
Institution records 1841–1966

Coventry Conservative Club records
1909–25

Coventry Liberal Club minutes 1873–9

Shut End estate, Kingswinford: records
17th–20th cent

Kingswinford manor court roll 1575–76

WJ Turney & Co Ltd, leather mfrs,
Stourbridge: deeds and papers 17th–20th
cent

National Society of Metal Mechanics,
Dudley branch: contribution registers
1948–75

South Staffordshire and East Worcestershire Educational Sustenance and South
Staffordshire, East Worcestershire and
Salop Miners Convalescent Homes
funds: records 1938–76

Stourbridge Firebrick Association and
Stourbridge and district Wages and
Conciliation Board for the Firebrick
Industry: records 19th–20th cent

WALSALL ARCHIVES SERVICE, LOCAL
HISTORY CENTRE, ESSEX STREET,
WALSALL WS2 7AS

Jesson family of West Bromwich:
corresp etc 18th–20th cent

Orgills Laundry Ltd, Walsall: records
20th cent

Walsall Football Club Ltd: records
1920–87

Walsall and Darlaston Methodist Circuit:
further records 19th–20th cent

WOLVERHAMPTON BOROUGH ARCHIVES,
CENTRAL LIBRARY, SNOW HILL,
WOLVERHAMPTON WV1 3AX

Terence John Pitt (1937–1986),
politician: papers

Goodyear Tyre & Rubber Co (Great
Britain) Ltd: records c1920–87

Henry Rogers, Sons & Co Ltd, hardware
merchants, Wolverhampton: further
records 1858–91

Amalgamated Union of Engineering
Workers: John Thompson Motor
Pressings Ltd, Wolverhampton, works
committee minutes 1919–86

National Society of Metal Mechanics,
Wolverhampton branch: contribution
books 20th cent

Wolverhampton Teachers Association
records 1903–78

NORFOLK

NORFOLK RECORD OFFICE,
CENTRAL LIBRARY, BETHEL STREET,
NORWICH NR2 1NJ

Carleton family of Norwich: papers
1772–1914

Cresswell family of Kings Lynn: family
papers 1824–1907

Norgate family of Sparham: papers
16th–20th cent

Upcher family of Sheringham Hall:
family and estate papers 17th–20th cent

Richard Corbet, bishop of Norwich:
synodical address rel to benevolence for
St Paul's Cathedral 1634

Doreen Wallace, novelist: letters to Roy
Winstanley 1957–71

Stanley John Wearing, architect,
Norwich: papers 1900–48

Arthur Bensly Whittingham: papers as
surveyor to Norwich Cathedral and
family papers c1830–1980, incl papers of
WT Bensly, chapter clerk

Diss deeds 1369–1557

Buxton Levishaw, Lammas and Oxnead
Hall manorial records 17th–20th cent;
court minutes of Sparham Hall in Necton
manor 1595–1602

Hayes & Storr, solicitors, Wells and
Fakenham: estate and other maps
1581–20th cent; survey books of Edward
Houghton, land surveyor, Wells
c1830–40

Richard Grand, blacksmith, Hackford:
accounts 1780–88

Holt deanery chapter minutes 1901–86

Norwich Primitive Methodist Circuit
records 1822–54

Benevolent Association for the relief of
decayed tradesmen, Norwich: records
1790–1961

NORTHAMPTONSHIRE

NORTHAMPTONSHIRE RECORD OFFICE,
DELAPRÉ ABBEY, LONDON ROAD,
NORTHAMPTON NN4 9AW

Parish records of Greens Norton
1565–1978, Lilford 1560–1985, Pilton
1569–1837 and Thorpe Achurch
1591–1837

Kettering Road Unitarian Church,
Northampton: records 1826–1949

Daventry and district Trades Council
records 1964–86

NORTHUMBERLAND

NORTHUMBERLAND RECORD OFFICE,
MELTON PARK, NORTH GOSFORTH,
NEWCASTLE UPON TYNE NE3 5QX

Allgood family of Nunwick: further
estate papers 18th–19th cent

Browne family of Callaly Castle: estate
papers c1900–87

Delaval family, baronets, of Seaton
Delaval: further estate papers, incl
Hartley glassworks records 1760–1890

Hall family of Otterburn Tower: deeds
and papers 17th–19th cent

Middleton family, baronets, of Belsay
Castle: further estate papers 18th–20th
cent

Ridley family of Park End, Simonburn:
estate papers 1898–1945

Charles Alderson & Son, solicitors,
Morpeth: deeds and papers 17th–20th
cent

Ashington colliery: railway traffic
records 20th cent

RG Bolam & Son, land agents,
Rothbury: records 1780–1960

Church of Scotland: records for Belford
1776–1848, St Andrew's, Berwick upon
Tweed 1780–1978 and Lowick
1804–1984 churches

United Reformed Church: records for
Belford 1820–1972, Harbottle
1803–1979, Longframlington
1754–1976, St George's, Morpeth
1721–1955 and Thropton 1799–1978
churches

National Union of Mineworkers,
Northumberland area: corresp with
branches 1940–80

North of England Institute of Mining
and Mechanical Engineers: records rel to
mining industry, incl those of London
Lead Co 1692–1899

Northumberland Coal Owners
Association (addnl): county agreements
1891–1947

Durham and Northumberland Mines
Rescue Station: daily occurrence books
1913–68

River Coquet Fishery Board minutes
1921–50

River Tweed Bridge Trust records
1884–1985

NOTTINGHAMSHIRE

NOTTINGHAMSHIRE ARCHIVES OFFICE,
COUNTY HOUSE, HIGH PAVEMENT,
NOTTINGHAM NG1 1HR

Darwin family of Elston: further deeds
17th–19th cent

Lander and Meads families of Chilwell
and Alrewas, Staffordshire: papers
c1700–1940

Alfred H Howe & Son, lace curtain mfrs,
Nottingham: accounts etc c1922–32

Newstead Colliery records c1890–1986

Pearson Bros Ltd, department store,
Nottingham: records 19th–20th cent

James Peacock Educational Foundation,
Ruddington: records 1667–1964

OXFORDSHIRE

OXFORDSHIRE COUNTY RECORD OFFICE,
COUNTY HALL, NEW ROAD,
OXFORD OX1 1ND

Morrell family of Headington Hill Hall:
further family papers 19th cent

Munsey family of Oxford: family papers
20th cent

Bullingdon hundred court roll 1428–29

Home Farm, Grafton: records 18th–20th
cent

WH Brakspear & Sons Ltd, brewers,
Henley: further records 19th–20th cent

George Coggins, solicitor, Deddington:
records 1868–1921

Oxford Provident Building Society:
records 19th–20th cent

Methodist Circuit records for Chipping
Norton and Stow 19th–20th cent and
Witney and Faringdon 20th cent

Witney monthly meeting, Society of
Friends: further records 19th–20th cent

Lord Williams School, Thame: records
19th–20th cent

Electrical Association for Women,
Banbury branch: minutes 20th cent

National Register of Archives, Oxford
committee: records 20th cent

SHROPSHIRE

SHROPSHIRE RECORD OFFICE, SHIREHALL,
ABBEY FOREGATE, SHREWSBURY SY2 6ND

Broughton-Adderley family of Tunstall
Hall: further deeds and estate papers
1321–1836

Dovaston family of West Felton: deeds
17th–20th cent

Edstaston Hall deeds 1725–1899

TS & D Evans, tanners, Oswestry:
accounts 1884–1934

Wace, Morgan & Salt, solicitors,
Shrewsbury: records 1923–71

Turton charity, Whitchurch: records
1794–20th cent

SOMERSET

SOMERSET RECORD OFFICE, OBRIDGE
ROAD, TAUNTON TA2 7PU

Duckworth family of Orchardleigh
(addnl): family papers 19th cent

Herbert family, Earls of Carnarvon
(addnl): family papers late 19th–20th
cent, incl further personal and political
corresp of Aubrey Herbert MP c1902–23
and corresp of Evelyn, Viscountess de
Vesci 1874–1928

Taunton Co-operative Society Ltd:
minutes 1902–61

STAFFORDSHIRE

STAFFORDSHIRE RECORD OFFICE,
EASTGATE STREET, STAFFORD ST16 2LZ

Bridgeman family, Earls of Bradford
(addnl): Knockin, Salop estate records
18th–20th cent

Hodgson family of Swinscoe: deeds and
papers 1767–1841

Walter Chetwynd, antiquary:
Chetwyndorum Stemma (cartulary), 1690

Heath House estate, Tean: deeds and
estate papers 18th–20th cent

Manor court books for Longdon
1882–1936, Cannock and Rugeley and
Haywood 1872–1940

JD Bebbington, estate agent, Endon:
papers rel to Staffs estates 1804–1979

Birmingham Railway Carriage &
Wagon Co Ltd (addnl): records
1855–1948

William Ward, iron and coal master,
Priestfield colliery: memorandum and
account book 1812–48

Bradley Endowed School Trust records 1563–1975

Cannock Conduit Trust records 1735–1943

Standon Home Guard records 1940–44

Holt Wilson family of Nowton and Bury St Edmunds: estate accounts 1775–83 and misc papers 1891–1944

Groton Hall manor rental 1525 and court rolls 1613–1762

Amalgamated Union of Building Trade Workers, Lichfield branch: records 20th cent

Trentham Ruridecanal Association minute books 1843–1970

Furneaux Hall Farm, Whatfield: accounts 1917–44

Polstead watermill day book 1921–23

Silverstreet Farm, Withersfield: accounts 1939–47

William Wentley, joiner, Newmarket: ledger 1797–1803

SUFFOLK

Cornwallis family, Marquesses Cornwallis (addnl): Norfolk and Suffolk manorial records 1272–1840, ministers accounts 1408–1577, household accounts 1555–1789, accounts of Sir Thomas Cornwallis as treasurer of Calais 1555–57 and letter book of Charles, 1st Marquess Cornwallis, as governor-general of Bengal 1787 (Iveagh collection)

Phillipps MSS: Suffolk collections, incl records of religious houses, heraldic and antiquarian papers, manorial records and deeds c1116–mid 19th cent (Iveagh collection)

Stanley Smith, local historian, Ipswich: working papers 20th cent

Court books for the manors of Kettlebers in Cretingham 1640–1714 and Redgrave with Botesdale and Gislingham 1681–95

Flick & Son, auctioneers, Saxmundham: records 1868–1952

Ransomes & Rapier plc, crane and excavator mfrs, Ipswich: records 1869–1986

Red Sleeve Charity, Ipswich: further records 1881–1982

Trinity House, Ipswich: records 1955–80

British and Foreign Bible Society, Bury St Edmunds and district auxiliary: minutes 1872–1966

Mary Ann Butts, midwife, Lowestoft: case registers 1908–15

Eastern Coach Works Ltd, omnibus mfrs, Lowestoft: records c1930–80

Transferred from Suffolk RO, Ipswich:

Edmund Gillingwater, topographer, and Robert Reeve: MS history of Mutford and Lothingland 1795–1807

Mutford and Lothingland hundred manorial records 13th–20th cent

Bungay Town Trust: deeds of Bungay town lands and Bungay Grammar School 1561–1904

Oulton Poor Land Trustees records 1858–1969

Outney Common Owners, Bungay: records 1655–1974

SURREY

SURREY RECORD OFFICE,
COUNTY HALL, PENRHYN ROAD,
KINGSTON UPON THAMES KT1 2DN

Heath family of Moorhurst, Dorking: deeds and papers 19th cent

John Westcott, Baptist schoolmaster: account book 1852–72

Epsom Grand Stand Association Ltd: records 1829–1969

Reigate Industrial & Provident (Co-operative) Society Ltd: minutes 1863–67

Dorking Charities Trustees: records 1675–1945

Rutlish Foundation, Merton: records 1753–1987

SURREY RECORD OFFICE,
GUILDFORD MUNIMENT ROOM,
CASTLE ARCH, GUILDFORD GU1 3SX

Webb family of Milford House: family and estate papers 1510–1911

Augusta Mary Brodrick, Viscountess Midleton: diaries 1855–98

Onslow Village Ltd, Guildford: records 1919–82

Farnham borough and parish records 1247–20th cent

Chertsey Street Baptist Chapel, Guildford: records 1713–1953

Archbishop Abbot's Exhibition Foundation, Guildford: records 1856–1980, incl Archbishop Abbot's School records 1856–1933

EAST SUSSEX

EAST SUSSEX RECORD OFFICE,
THE MALTINGS, CASTLE PRECINCTS,
LEWES BN7 1YT

Blencowe family of The Hook, Chailey: further diaries 1830–99

Gilbert family of Trelissick, Cornwall and Eastbourne: further estate papers rel to development of Eastbourne 1861–20th cent

Grantham family of Chailey (addnl): family and estate papers 1809–20th cent

Molineux family of Isfield: family and estate papers 19th–20th cent

John Burgess of Ditchling: journal 1785–90 and letters from America 1794–1815

Thomas Cooper of New Place, Guestling: account book 1788–1824

Richard Stileman, magistrate, Winchelsea: notebook 1819–26

Manor court rolls and records for Brightling Prebend 1624–1804; Brighton 1699–1875; Bucksteep 1422–25; Pashley 1820–75; Sapperton 1663–1775; Sprivers in Horsmonden, Kent 1718–1821 and Wartling 1431–44

Andrews & Bennett, solicitors, Burwash: clients papers 16th–20th cent

Brook family of Church Farm, Bexhill: accounts 1730–1917

R Butler & Sons, undertakers, Hailsham: ledger 1917–25

F&J Tooth, timber merchants, Brighton: records 1850–58

PO Tooth, wine and spirit merchants, Brighton: records 1849–58

WEST SUSSEX

WEST SUSSEX RECORD OFFICE,
COUNTY HALL, CHICHESTER PO19 1RN

Fletcher family of Aldwick: legal papers 1786–1938

Richard Cobden MP (addnl): letters to Sir Joshua Walmsley MP 1848–57

John Walter Atherton Hussey (1909–1985), dean of Chichester: corresp and papers

Strood Park, Slinfold: deeds and estate papers c1250–1715

Memoranda book of Shermanbury and
Ewhurst manors c1887–1908

Allan family, farmers: accounts rel to
farms at Romsey, Hants 1876–95
and Trotton 1895–1944

Robert Allen, jeweller, Chichester:
accounts 1937–67

Walter Bros Ltd, drapers, Worthing:
business and family papers 1846–1971

Chichester Cycling Club records
1878–1950

East Grinstead Labour Party minutes
1918–70

*Transferred from Sussex Archaeological
Society:*

Warnham deeds 13th cent–1620

Rowley manor court minutes and rentals
16th–17th cent

TYNE AND WEAR

TYNE AND WEAR ARCHIVES SERVICE,
BLANDFORD HOUSE,
WEST BLANDFORD STREET,
NEWCASTLE UPON TYNE NE1 4JA

Shafto family of Benwell: estate papers
1538–1925, incl Benwell manor records
1632–1901 (transferred from
Northumberland RO)

Sherlock and Scott families of Tynemouth: papers 1791–1976

Wilson family of Forest Hall: family and
estate papers 16th–20th cent (transferred
from Northumberland RO)

George HJ Daysh, geographer: papers on
industrial development in the North-
East and Cumberland 1925–65

George S Eskdale (1897–1960),
trumpeter: papers

A McGreehan, diver: papers 1919–56

Nicholas Wood and other colliery
viewers: reports 1736–1839

Legge & Miller, solicitors, Houghton-le-
Spring (addnl): clients papers 18th–20th
cent

East Coast Timber Co Ltd, Sunderland:
records 1921–86

English Industrial Estates Corporation,
Team Valley (addnl): records 1936–86

Hetton Race Co Ltd and Houghton
Greyhound Stadium Club: records
1914–70

E Jopling & Sons Ltd, steel castings mfrs,
Sunderland: records 1897–1982

R & RF Kidd, solicitors, North Shields:
records 19th–20th cent

J & W Lowry Ltd, builders and
contractors, Newcastle: records
1887–1980

Northern Sound Services, recording
agency, Newcastle: records 1948–86

North Shields Fish Meal & Oil Co Ltd:
records 1949–76

Bethesda Methodist Chapel, Gateshead:
records from 1836

United Reformed Church: records of St
Paul's and St John's Church, South
Shields 1744–1986 and of St George's
with Trinity and St James Church,
Sunderland (addnl) 1822–1963; Sunderland Congregational churches 1832–1966
(transferred from Durham RO)

George Hudson's Charity, Sunderland:
records 19th–20th cent

South Shields Marine College records
from 1862

Sunderland Orphanage and Educational
Foundation records 19th–20th cent

Newcastle Lying-In Hospital (addnl):
admissions register 1760–81

National and Local Government Officers
Association, Gateshead branch: records
1934–80

Transport and General Workers Union,
Newcastle region: further records
1932–85

United Pattern Makers Association, Jarrow and Newcastle East branches: records 1892–1972

Incorporation of Butchers, Newcastle (addnl): records 1897–1986

Incorporation of Sailmakers, Newcastle (addnl): corresp 1812–28

Electrical Association for Women, Whitley Bay and Newcastle branches: records 1960–83

International Order of Good Templars, Olive Branch lodge, North Shields: records 1872–1982

Newcastle and Gateshead Choral Union records 1888–1984

Northumberland Park Bowling Club records 1889–1986

Tynemouth district and Whitley Bay Trades Council records 1951–74

WARWICKSHIRE

WARWICK COUNTY RECORD OFFICE,
PRIORY PARK, CAPE ROAD,
WARWICK CV34 4JS

Craven family, Earls of Craven: further deeds and estate papers 1721–1928

Tarlton family of Hall End Farm, Ullenhall: deeds and estate papers 1552–20th cent

W Botterill, engineer, Rugby: papers rel to service in Egypt, India and Ceylon 1900–34

TR Allen, grocer, Studley: records c1877–90

Samuel Davy & Son, auctioneers and estate agents, Knowle: records 20th cent

Electrical Association for Women, Nuneaton and Rugby branches: minutes 1973–85

Kenilworth Female Friendly Society records 1826–1973

Warwickshire Natural History and Archaeology Society records from 1836

SHAKESPEARE BIRTHPLACE TRUST
RECORDS OFFICE,
THE SHAKESPEARE CENTRE,
STRATFORD-UPON-AVON CV37 6QW

Verney family, Barons Willoughby de Broke: further deeds and estate papers 1595–1965

Marie Corelli, novelist (addnl): letters (16) to AMN Greenwood 1922–23

Walker Barnard, auctioneers and valuers, Stratford-upon-Avon: records 1919–59

Frank Organ Ltd, house furnishers, Stratford-upon-Avon: records 1868–1983

TN Waldron Ltd, metal stampers, Birmingham and Stratford-upon-Avon: records 1910–56

Warwickshire County Garage, Stratford-upon-Avon (addnl): records 1910–79

King Edward's School, Stratford-upon-Avon (addnl): governors minutes 1900–55

Swan of Avon Masonic Lodge (addnl): records 1887–1959

ISLE OF WIGHT

ISLE OF WIGHT COUNTY RECORD OFFICE,
26 HILLSIDE, NEWPORT PO30 2EB

Landguard estate, Shanklin: deeds 1552–1749

Buckell & Drew, solicitors, Newport (addnl): Newport and Carisbrooke deeds 1666–1896

Damant & Sons, solicitors, Cowes: West Cowes deeds 1768–1863

James Eldridge & Sons, solicitors, Newport: deeds 1698–1964

WB Mew, Langton & Co Ltd, brewers, Newport: partnership agreements and title deeds 1830–1900

Way, Riddett, estate agents, Newport: further records 1850–1950

Arreton Charity Trust records
1784–1956

B Company, 20th (East Wight) Bn,
Hampshire Home Guard: records
1940–44

WILTSHIRE

WILTSHIRE RECORD OFFICE,
COUNTY HALL, TROWBRIDGE BA14 8JG

Beckett family of Westbury: deeds and
estate papers 17th–19th cent

Bourne family of Melksham, wine
merchants and grocers: records
1760–1800

Pleydell-Bouverie family, Earls of
Radnor: further Longford estate papers
16th cent–1966

Newton Toney manor survey 1795

PJ Parmiter & Sons Ltd, agricultural
engineers, Tisbury: records 1917–75

Mid-Wiltshire Methodist Circuit records
1775–1980

Amalgamated Engineering Union,
Swindon branch records c1920–70

Wiltshire chambers of commerce records
c1880–1970

Country Landowners Association, Wilt-
shire branch records 20th cent

Kingsdown Golf Club, Box: records
1890–1972

Swindon Athletic Club records
1890–1960

NORTH YORKSHIRE

NORTH YORKSHIRE COUNTY RECORD
OFFICE, COUNTY HALL,
NORTHALLERTON DL7 8AD

Denys family, baronets, of Draycott Hall
(addnl): family and estate papers
1796–1923, incl Irish and American estate
and business papers 1796–1901

Palmer family, baronets, of Grinkle
Park: family and estate papers 1715–1957

Wentworth-Fitzwilliam family, Earls
Fitzwilliam: further Malton estate papers
1719–1938, incl Derwent Navigation
accounts 1805–55

Hurst lead mining accounts 1660–68

Rye Internal Drainage Board records
c1930–52

YORK CITY ARCHIVES DEPARTMENT,
ART GALLERY BUILDING,
EXHIBITION SQUARE, YORK YO1 2EW

Ware & Co, solicitors, York: deeds and
papers, mainly 18th–20th cent, incl
Harland family of Sutton Hall

SOUTH YORKSHIRE

BARNSLEY ARCHIVE SERVICE,
CENTRAL LIBRARY, SHAMBLES STREET,
BARNSLEY S70 2FJ

Roy Mason (b1924), Baron Mason:
papers (some transferred from Sheffield
RO)

Thurlstone inclosure agreement 1750

Lancasters, chartered surveyors,
Barnsley: valuation books 1829–63;
Cannon Hall and Wentworth Castle
estate papers 19th–20th cent

Clarkson's Old Brewery (Barnsley) Ltd:
barrelage book 1930–57

Goldthorpe Collieries Ltd, Rotherham:
check weighmans committee minute
book 1911–20

Barnsley Methodist Circuit (addnl):
minutes 1923–81

Barnsley Citizens Advice Bureau records
c1963–80

Shaw Lands Trust records c1900–85

West Riding of Yorkshire Miners
Permanent Relief Fund Friendly Society:
further records 1877–1987

DONCASTER ARCHIVES DEPARTMENT,
KING EDWARD ROAD, BALBY,
DONCASTER DN4 0NA

Tudworth Grange Farm, Hatfield: deeds
1656–1863

Armthorpe inclosure award and map
1774 (transferred from W Yorks RO)

Rye & Leman, solicitors, London: deeds
and estate papers rel to properties in
Hatfield and Thorne, incl Dunscroft
manor court books

Peglers Ltd, brass founders, Doncaster:
records 1886–1983

Doncaster Constituency Labour Party:
further records 1948–74

BRIAN O'MALLEY CENTRAL LIBRARY,
WALKER PLACE, ROTHERHAM S65 1JH

Rotherham inclosure award 1764

George Wright (Rotherham) Ltd, ironfounders: records c1850–1960

Church of Our Father (Unitarian),
Rotherham: records 18th cent–1987

Association of Yorkshire Bookmen,
Rotherham branch: records 1944–78

SHEFFIELD RECORD OFFICE,
CENTRAL LIBRARY, SURREY STREET,
SHEFFIELD S1 1XZ

Alfred O Elmhirst, farmer, of
Worsbrough Bridge (addnl): papers 20th
cent

Newton, Chambers & Co Ltd, ironfounders, Thorncliffe: further records
19th–20th cent

Charles Ross Ltd, structural engineers,
Sheffield: further records 20th cent

Sheffield & South Yorkshire Navigation
Co records 20th cent

Joseph Smith & Sons (Timber
Merchants) Ltd: deeds and financial
records c1830–1950

Howard Hill (North of England) Girls
Reformatory: records c1860–90

Association of Scientific Technical and
Managerial Staff, Sheffield branch:
records 1959–70

National Union of Teachers, Sheffield
Association: minutes 1887–1984

Hallamshire Accident Compensation
Society: records 1897–1985

Sheffield Temperance Association
records 1863–1927

Birley and Gleadless Ward Labour Party:
minutes 1953–79

WEST YORKSHIRE

WEST YORKSHIRE ARCHIVE SERVICE
HEADQUARTERS, REGISTRY OF DEEDS,
NEWSTEAD ROAD, WAKEFIELD WF1 2DE

Beetham family of Ackworth: papers
c1872–1957

Frank Green, colliery engineer: papers
c1890–1907

Croda Hydrocarbons Ltd, Knottingley:
records 1878–1955

Halifax Building Society, Horbury
branch: records 1714–1943

Ralph Sweeting, solicitor, Wakefield:
records c1843–1968

National Union of Teachers,
Hemsworth and South Elmsall
association: records 1929–74

Childrens International Summer
Villages: records 1962–84

Castleford Labour Party records 1944–74

WEST YORKSHIRE ARCHIVE SERVICE,
BRADFORD DISTRICT ARCHIVES,
15 CANAL ROAD, BRADFORD BD1 4AT

Salt family, baronets: papers 1877–1910,
incl records of Saltaire Institute

Kenneth Preston of Keighley: family
papers 1918–85

Atkin & Co, textile mfrs, Bradford: records 1881–1951

Salts (Saltaire) Ltd, worsted spinners: records 20th cent

Taylor Bros (Waterloo Mills) Ltd, yarn spinners, Silsden: records 1882–1976

Wibsey Wesleyan Reform Church records 1833–1983

St Andrew's Society, Bradford branch: records 1886–1986

Bradford Independent Labour Party records 1910–68

WEST YORKSHIRE ARCHIVE SERVICE, CALDERDALE DISTRICT ARCHIVES, CENTRAL LIBRARY, NORTHGATE HOUSE, HALIFAX HX1 1UN

S Appleyard & Co, machine tool mfrs, Halifax: records c1898–1953

Automatic Standard Screw Co (Halifax) Ltd, bolt mfrs: records 1848–1914

JC Bottomley & Emerson Ltd, paint, varnish and dye mfrs, Brighouse: records 1878–1979

Wilson & Thomas, solicitors, Todmorden: records c1592–1930

Ogden Mount Zion Methodist Chapel records 1775–1985

National Union of Dyers, Bleachers and Textile Workers, Greetland branch: records 1919–82

WEST YORKSHIRE ARCHIVE SERVICE, KIRKLEES DISTRICT ARCHIVES, CENTRAL LIBRARY, PRINCESS ALEXANDRA WALK, HUDDERSFIELD HD1 2SU

Cousen family of Huddersfield: papers 1664–1912

William Wilks, surgeon, Huddersfield: personal and family papers 1781–1970

Bent Ley Silk Mills Ltd, Meltham: records 1848–1904

D Skippins & Son, joiners and undertakers, Dewsbury: accounts 1938–77

Slaithwaite Methodist Circuit records 1833–1973

WEST YORKSHIRE ARCHIVE SERVICE, LEEDS DISTRICT ARCHIVES, CHAPELTOWN ROAD, SHEEPSCAR, LEEDS LS7 3AP

N Chambers, corn merchant, Leeds: records 1930–39

Scholefield, Taylor & Maggs, solicitors, Batley: records 19th–20th cent

Yorkshire Indigo Scarlet & Colour Dyers Ltd, Leeds: records 1945–59

Rothwell Holy Trinity parish records 1538–20th cent

Leeds Charity School: further records 1669–1882

Designer Makers North and Guild of Yorkshire Craftsmen: records c1970–87

British and Foreign Bible Society, Leeds auxiliary: records 1945–86

WEST YORKSHIRE ARCHIVE SERVICE, YORKSHIRE ARCHAEOLOGICAL SOCIETY, CLAREMONT, 23 CLARENDON ROAD, LEEDS LS2 9NZ

Leeds Freemasons, Defence Lodge No 1221: minutes 1879–1976

Local Repositories: Wales

CLWYD

CLWYD RECORD OFFICE,
THE OLD RECTORY, HAWARDEN,
DEESIDE CH5 3NR

Charles Edward Evans (1873–1963), journalist: corresp and papers

Edward Ratcliffe, boilermaker, Hawarden: accounts 1876–85

Wern Colliery, Bagillt: accounts 1875–79

CLWYD RECORD OFFICE,
46 CLWYD STREET,
RUTHIN LL15 1HP

Denbigh lordship court of estrays: records 1851–1983

S Aston & Son Ltd, furniture mfrs, Wrexham: records 1900–74

Rhydleos mill, Llansilin: accounts 1854–57

Bethlehem Independent Chapel, Rhosllanerchrugog: baptismal registers 1810–37

Council of Free Churches, Ruthin: records 1938–86

Wrexham Peripatetic Society records 1872–1936

Conservative Party: records of Denbighshire branches 1948–77

Denbigh and district Liberal Association minutes 1956–76

DYFED

DYFED ARCHIVE SERVICE,
CARMARTHENSHIRE RECORD OFFICE,
COUNTY HALL, CARMARTHEN SA31 1JP

Pemberton family of Llanelli: deeds and estate papers 18th–19th cent, incl Carnawllon commote rental 1704

Merthyr Unity Philanthropic Institution, Blodeuon Glanfferws lodge records 20th cent

DYFED ARCHIVE SERVICE,
PEMBROKESHIRE RECORD OFFICE,
THE CASTLE, HAVERFORDWEST SA61 2EF

Oliver Cromwell: corresp with Haverfordwest Corporation rel to the castle 1648

Evans family of Cilgerran, architects and shipowners: papers 1766–1880

Higgon family of Scolton: further family and estate papers 1737–1863 (transferred from the National L of Wales)

Hobbs family of Crunwere: papers 19th–20th cent

WH Martin, timber merchant, Haverfordwest: personal and business papers 20th cent

Bethesda Baptist Church, Haverfordwest: records 1787–1980

GLAMORGAN (MID, SOUTH AND WEST)

GLAMORGAN ARCHIVE SERVICE,
GLAMORGAN RECORD OFFICE,
COUNTY HALL, CATHAYS PARK,
CARDIFF CF1 3NE

Gwilim John Butler, schoolmaster: papers 20th cent

William Lewis of Hughesoffka, Ukraine: papers rel to New Russia Co Ltd 1880–95

David Sallis & Sons, hardware dealers, Bargoed: records 1928–49

South Wales Art Society (addnl): records 1948–80

Aberfan Disaster Enquiry: papers of
RJ Piggott and K Wardell 1966–67

GLAMORGAN ARCHIVE SERVICE,
WEST GLAMORGAN AREA RECORD OFFICE,
COUNTY HALL, OYSTERMOUTH ROAD,
SWANSEA SA1 3SN

Glasbrook family of Swansea: deeds
1860–1951

Rice-Evans family of Eaglebush,
Neath: deeds and papers 17th–20th
cent

Captain Hector Leighton Davies:
papers rel to steel and tinplate
industry 1908–67

Prince of Wales Dry Dock Co,
Swansea Ltd and subsidiaries (addnl):
records 1897–1971

Yniscedwyn Iron, Steel & Coal Co
Ltd: deeds 1837–83

GWENT

GWENT RECORD OFFICE, COUNTY HALL,
CWMBRAN NP44 2XH

Winsloe family of Trelleck: deeds
1701–1910

Crawshay Bailey (1785–1872) MP: deeds
of his Glamorgan and Monmouth-
shire estates c1716–1926

William Watkins, farmer, Llantilio
Pertholey: farm diary 1851–64

Court Farm, Dingestow: diaries and
accounts 1829–1926

Ebbw Vale Steel, Iron & Coal Co Ltd:
colliery pay books 1875–81

GWYNEDD

GWYNEDD ARCHIVES SERVICE,
CAERNARFON AREA RECORD OFFICE,
COUNTY OFFICES, CAERNARFON LL55 1SH

Thomas family of Beddgelert: family
papers 1866–1953

Watkin family of Murian, Criccieth:
family and estate papers 1822–1918

Lt–Commander Thomas Pritchard:
memoirs at Stanley internment camp,
Hong Kong 1941–44

Henry Thomas, homoeopathic
physician, Llandudno: corresp and
papers rel to his medical qualifi-
cations and their recognition 1852–83

Cefnamlwch estate: further deeds
1527–1814

WS Barker and DL Bloor, ironmongers, Llanfairfechan: records
1929–74

John C Jones, house furnisher,
Pwllheli: records 1909–67

I Isgoed Williams, architect and
surveyor, Penmaenmawr: drawings
and papers 20th cent

Welsh Agricultural Organisation
Society Ltd: records rel to
Caernarfonshire c1940–80

GWYNEDD ARCHIVES SERVICE,
DOLGELLAU AREA RECORD OFFICE,
CAE PENARLAG, DOLGELLAU LL40 2YB

Peniarth estate, Llanegryn: corresp
and deeds 1827–1914

Penmaenucha estate, Penmaenpool:
further records 19th–20th cent

Rhagatt estate, Corwen: further
papers 18th–19th cent

Dolgellau Golf Club: further
records 19th–20th cent

GWYNEDD ARCHIVES SERVICE,
LLANGEFNI AREA RECORD OFFICE,
SHIRE HALL, LLANGEFNI LL77 7TW

Evan Madoc Jones, teacher, Beaumaris:
further papers

Rhuddgaer estate: further papers
19th–20th cent

POWYS

LIBRARIES AND MUSEUMS DEPARTMENT,
COUNTY LIBRARY HEADQUARTERS,
CEFNLLYS ROAD,
LLANDRINDOD WELLS LD1 5LD

Baskerville family of Clyro Court: estate papers 1682–1926

Lewis Lloyd family of Nantgwyllt, Rhayader: deeds and papers 1548–1973, incl Grange of Cwmteuddwr manor presentments 1722–1817

Robertson Williams family of Plas Pantsaison: Brecon and Pembs deeds and family papers 1728–1948 (transferred from Dyfed Archives, Haverfordwest)

Llandinam estate accounts 1891–1944

Pen Ithon estate papers 1868–1903

Local Repositories: Scotland

CENTRAL

CENTRAL REGIONAL COUNCIL ARCHIVES
DEPARTMENT, OLD HIGH SCHOOL,
SPITTAL STREET, STIRLING FK8 1DG

Graham family of Cassafuir and Ruskie, Perthshire: family and estate papers c1691–1830

Norrieston, Perthshire, cartulary 1716–1849

James Gray & Co Ltd, seed and manure merchants, Stirling: records late 19th cent–c1970

Stirling Gas Light Co: records c1900–46

DUMFRIES AND GALLOWAY

DUMFRIES ARCHIVE CENTRE,
33 BURNS STREET, DUMFRIES DG1 2PS

Maitland family of Valleyfield: family and estate papers 19th cent

Stewart family of Shambellie: family and estate papers 16th–20th cent

Dalbeattie Co-operative Society records 1860–90

Dumfries Methodist Church records 1796–1968

Dumfries Industrial School records 1750–1973

Scottish Typographical Association, Dumfries branch: minutes 1831–1979

Admiralty court, barony of Logan and Clanyard: minute book 1788–1806

LOTHIAN

CITY OF EDINBURGH DISTRICT COUNCIL
ARCHIVES,
DEPARTMENT OF ADMINISTRATION,
CITY CHAMBERS, HIGH STREET,
EDINBURGH EH1 1YJ

Wood family: corresp and papers 18th–19th cent

Gideon Walker Ltd, wood flour mfrs: records 1873–1940

STRATHCLYDE

STRATHCLYDE REGIONAL ARCHIVES,
MITCHELL LIBRARY, 201 NORTH STREET,
GLASGOW G3 7DN

Cochrane-Baillie family, Barons Lamington: family and estate papers 15th–20th cent

Shaw-Stewart family, baronets, of
Greenock and Blackhall: further
Ardgowan estate papers 19th–20th cent

J & T Boyd, textile machinery mfrs,
Glasgow: further records 20th cent

Glasgow Stevedores Association records
1898–1975

Scottish Engineering Employers
Association records *c*1912–73

ARGYLL AND BUTE DISTRICT ARCHIVES,
KILMORY, LOCHGILPHEAD PA31 8RT

Minard estate: plans book 1839

TAYSIDE

DUNDEE DISTRICT ARCHIVE AND RECORD
CENTRE, CITY CHAMBERS, CITY SQUARE,
DUNDEE DD1 3BY

Carnegie family, Earls of Northesk:
Ethie estate papers 13th cent–1922 (transferred from Scottish RO)

James Cowan & Sons (Salt) Ltd, salt
merchants, Dundee: minutes 1954–66

Creasey, Son & Wickenden, chartered
accountants, Tunbridge Wells: corresp
with firms in Angus 1835–51

George Duncan & Co (Dundee) Ltd,
general merchants: minutes 1927–63

Dundee Supply Co Ltd, grocers: records
1887–1968

Victoria Spinning Co, jute spinners,
Dundee: wages books 1893–1971

Dundee Methodist Church records
1785–1980

Dundee, Perth and Blairgowrie
Methodist Circuit records 1839–1968

Dundee Orphan Institution records
1830–1969

Railway Clerks Association, Dundee
branch: records 1901–47

Dundee Industrial Schools Society
records 1859–1971

Dundee Society for the Prevention of
Cruelty to Animals: minutes 1896–1918

PERTH AND KINROSS DISTRICT ARCHIVE,
SANDEMAN LIBRARY,
16 KINNOULL STREET, PERTH PH1 5ET

Fergusson family of Balemund: family
and estate papers 1328–*c*1900

Electrical Association for Women, Perth
branch: records 1949–86

Local Repositories: Isle of Man

MANX MUSEUM LIBRARY,
KINGSWOOD GROVE, DOUGLAS,
ISLE OF MAN

Peel Gas Light Co records 1854–1955

Peel Waterworks records 1859–1939

II: Reports added to the National Register of Archives

The list notices Reports Nos 29615–30610 added to the National Register of Archives in 1987.

Appended is a short supplementary list of some of the more significant replacements and additions to existing reports received during the year.

Asterisks denote reports of which copies have also been sent to the British Library (Official Publications Library), the Bodleian Library Oxford, the University Library Cambridge, London University Institute of Historical Research, the John Rylands University Library of Manchester, the National Library of Scotland, the Scottish Record Office, the National Library of Wales and the Public Record Office of Northern Ireland.

Nos 29615–30610

29615 Mobberley Priory deeds (Phillipps MSS) 9pp *Cheshire RO*
29616 Henry Greenall & Co, solicitors, Warrington: clients papers 53pp *Cheshire RO*
29617 Northumberland Golf Club 1p *Tyne and Wear Archives Dept*
29618 Labour Party: Brecon and Radnor division 14pp *National L of Wales*
29619 Gateshead: Park Terrace Presbyterian Church 1p *Tyne and Wear Archives Dept*
29620 Greenside: Rockwood Mission Independent Evangelical Church 1p *Tyne and Wear Archives Dept*
29621 Lingfield Church of England School 1p *Surrey RO, Kingston*

29622 Esher and Walton petty sessions 2pp *Surrey RO, Kingston*
29623 Hiram Walker & Sons (Scotland) Ltd, whisky distillers, Dumbarton 19pp *Glasgow Univ Archives*
29624 Finnie & Co Ltd, wholesale ironmongers, Glasgow 3pp *Private*
29625 Cessna Fluid Power Ltd, hydraulic equipment mfrs, Glenrothes, Fife 3pp *Private*
29626 Fraserburgh Baptist Church, Aberdeenshire 3pp *Private*
29627 Clyde Combustions Ltd, heating equipment mfrs, Glasgow 5pp *Private*
29628 Leonard Grandison & Son, plasterers and cement workers, Peebles 10pp *Private*
29629 Cardowan Creameries Ltd, margarine mfrs, Glasgow 4pp *Private*
29630 Glasgow: Partick Baptist Church 3pp *Private*
29631 Cambuslang Baptist Church, Glasgow 3pp *Private*
29632 Great Wyrley Womens Co-operative Guild 1p *Walsall Archives*
29633 Sir Cliff Tibbits, mayor of Walsall: corresp and misc papers 5pp *Walsall Archives*
29634 Whitehouse, Cox & Co Ltd, leather goods mfrs, Walsall 4pp *Walsall Archives*
29635 David Etchells & Son Ltd, machine tool mfrs, Darlaston 4pp *Walsall Archives*

29636 Walsall: Pleck Methodist Church 1p *Walsall Archives*

29637 Sir Derrick Melville Dunlop, physician: corresp and papers 59pp *Edinburgh Univ Medical Archive Centre*

29638 GH Hackett Ltd, builders, Swanwick 27pp *Hants RO*

29639 Swansea Savings Bank 7pp *Glamorgan RO*

29640 Folkestone Waterworks Co 7pp *Kent AO, Folkestone*

29641 Colin Edward Cherry, professor of telecommunication: corresp and papers 42pp *Imperial Coll, London Univ*

29642 James Watson Munro, professor of zoology and applied entomology: corresp and papers 37pp *Imperial Coll, London Univ*

29643 James Dwyer McGee, professor of applied physics: corresp and papers 7pp *Imperial Coll, London Univ*

29644 Dennis Gabor, physicist: corresp and papers 84pp *Imperial Coll, London Univ*

29645 Erith and Dartford Lighterage Co Ltd, Kent 6pp *Private*

29646 Sir Andrew Crombie Ramsay, geologist: diaries, notebooks and corresp 33pp *Imperial Coll, London Univ*

29647 Edmund Vaughan Ltd, builders merchants, Maidstone 5pp *Private*

29648 Charles Arkcoll Ltd, wholesale grocers, Maidstone 11pp *Private*

29649 R Corben & Sons (Holdings) Ltd, builders, Maidstone 5pp *Private*

29650 Alfred Reader & Co Ltd, cricket ball mfrs, Teston, Kent 7pp *Private*

29651 Yorkshire Society of Friends: Yorkshire general meeting and York monthly meeting 34pp *Brotherton L, Leeds Univ*

29652 Carrington (formerly Smith) family, Barons Carrington: family and estate papers 25pp *Bucks RO and Private*

29653 Nugent (formerly Savage) family of Portaferry, co Down: family and estate papers 272pp *PRO of N Ireland*

29654 Labour Party: Bilston division 2pp *Wolverhampton Central L*

29655 Phythian family of Manchester: family and business papers 64pp *Manchester Central L*

29656 Daniel Adamson & Co Ltd, boiler makers, Dukinfield 1p *Greater Manchester RO*

29657 Lomas and Murgatroyd families of Manchester: corresp and papers 39pp *Manchester Central L*

29658 Manchester: Ardwick Bicycle Club 4pp *Manchester Central L*

29659 William Bailey & Co Ltd, heating and sanitary engineers, Manchester 10pp *Manchester Central L*

29660 Manchester Soroptimist International 2pp *Manchester Central L*

29661 Manchester Soroptimist Housing Association Ltd 4pp *Manchester Central L*

29662 HMT Lancastria Association 2pp *Private*

★29663 Buller of Morval: family and estate papers 93pp *Cornwall RO*

29664 Hawkins and Johnstone families of Trewithen: family and estate papers 163pp *Cornwall RO*

29665 Bradford Sanitary Association 1p *Bradford Univ L*

29666 Bradford Engineering Society 1p *Bradford Univ L*

29667 Bradford Typographical Society 3pp *Bradford Univ L*

29668 Reginald Rogers & Son, solicitors, Helston 176pp *Cornwall RO*

29669 Berkshire schools 5pp *Berks RO*

29670 Charlton Kings Church of England Mens Society 1p *Glos RO*

29671 Franklin & Jones, solicitors, Gloucester 1p *Glos RO*

29672 Cambridgeshire schools 10pp *Multiple locations*

29673 Cheshire schools 50pp *Multiple locations*

29674 Cornwall schools 50pp *Cornwall RO*

29675 W Wilkinson & Co, soap mfrs, Sowerby Bridge 1p *Calderdale District Archives*

29676 James Stafford Ltd, plumbers, Sowerby Bridge 1p *Calderdale District Archives*

29677 Howarth & Ridehalgh, solicitors, Ripponden 6pp *Calderdale District Archives*

29678 Knottingley Civic Society 21pp *W Yorks RO*

29679 Brierley: Burntwood Isolation Hospital 15pp *W Yorks RO*

29680 Halifax Hospital Management Committee 5pp *W Yorks RO*

29681 Leeds Baptist Ministers Fraternity 2pp *W Yorks RO*

29682 Bradford District Missionary Committee 3pp *W Yorks RO*

29683 Halifax rural deanery 4pp *W Yorks RO*

29684 Sir John Richardson, Arctic explorer: corresp 199pp *Scott Polar Research Inst, Cambridge*

29685 Wakefield: English Martyrs Roman Catholic Parish 2pp *W Yorks RO*

29686 Cliffe Hill Granite Co Ltd, Markfield 10pp *Leics RO*

29687 Market Harborough and District Hospital 1p *Leics RO*

29688 Samuel Buckley & Co Ltd, machine tool makers, Ashton-under-Lyne 2pp *Greater Manchester RO*

29689 Rutland Association for the Prosecution of Felons 7pp *Leics RO*

29690 Appleby Magna Particular Baptist Chapel 1p *Leics RO*

29691 William Jones, chartist: corresp and misc papers 7pp *Leics RO*

29692 Kirby Muxloe Players 5pp *Leics RO*

29693 Leicester and County Footwear Manufacturers Association 9pp *Leics RO*

29694 George Hattersley & Sons Ltd, textile machinery mfrs, Keighley 52pp *Bradford District Archives*

29695 Leeds masonic halls 7pp *Yorks Archaeol Soc*

29696 Ilkley Congregational Church 1p *Bradford District Archives*

29697 Ilkley: Wells Road Wesleyan Methodist Chapel 1p *Bradford District Archives*

29698 Bradford and County Conservative Club 5pp *Bradford District Archives*

29699 Shipley Textile Society 2pp *Bradford District Archives*

29700 Baildon Urban District Council 2pp *Bradford District Archives*

29701 Wakefield Metropolitan District Council 60pp *W Yorks RO*

29702 Craven, Jowett & Son, printers, Bradford 1p *Bradford District Archives*

29703 Glyn Hughes, author: literary MSS 10pp *Bradford District Archives*

29704 Miriam Lord, teacher and educationist: corresp and papers 104pp *Bradford District Archives*

29705 Labour Party: Radstock branch 1p *Bristol Univ L*

29706 Leicester Trinity Methodist Circuit 6pp *Leics RO*

29707 Leicestershire Golf Club 57pp *Leics RO and Private*

29708 Mortimer family of Caldwell, Derbys, and Toppingo, Hatfield Peveril, Essex: family and estate papers 35pp *Leics RO*

29709 Leicestershire schools 4pp *Leics RO*

29710 William Vaughan Jones, playwright and antiquary: papers 20pp *Gwynedd Archives Service, Caernarfon*

29711 National Farmers Union: Caernarfonshire branch 35pp *Gwynedd Archives Service, Caernarfon*

29712 London: Wigmore Hall 4pp *Westminster Archives Dept, Marylebone*

29713 Typographical Association: Bradford branch 3pp *Bradford District Archives*

29714 Bradford: Dudley Hill Wesleyan Chapel 1p *Bradford District Archives*

29715 Yorkshire schools 1p *Multiple locations*

29716 Coventry Chain Co: shop stewards committee 4pp *Warwick Univ L*

29717 Sir Leslie Cannon, trade union official: corresp and papers 4pp *Warwick Univ L*

29718 John Blackburn, shoddy mfrs, Old Mill, Batley 1p *Kirklees District Archives*

29719 Golcar: Providence Methodist New Connexion Chapel 2pp *Kirklees District Archives*

29720 Thomas Bugbird & Son Ltd, civil engineers, Caernarfon 14pp *Gwynedd Archives Service, Caernarfon*

29721 Bulkeley Johnson family of Ysbyty: estate papers 15pp *Gwynedd Archives Service, Caernarfon*

29722 Sprott, Stokes & Turnbull, solicitors, Shrewsbury: Caerns deeds and papers 34pp *Gwynedd Archives Service, Caernarfon*

29723 St George's Steamship Co Ltd, Conway 22pp *Gwynedd Archives Service, Caernarfon*

29724 Samuel Richards, consulting quarry engineer, Llanberis 36pp *Gwynedd Archives Service, Caernarfon*

29725 John Lewis Williams, dispensing chemist and optician, Pwllheli: local history and other papers 26pp *Gwynedd Archives Service, Caernarfon*

29726 Evans family of Penarfynydd, Llanfaelrhys: misc papers 28pp *Gwynedd Archives Service, Caernarfon*

29727 Llandwrog: Brynrhos Calvinistic Methodist Chapel 19pp *Gwynedd Archives Service, Caernarfon*

★29728 John William Sutton Pringle, zoologist: corresp and papers 136pp *Bodleian L, Oxford*

29729 Spenborough Engineering Society 4pp *Kirklees District Archives*

29730 Samuel Vyvyan Trerice Adams, politician: corresp and papers 6pp *British L of Polit and Econ Science*

29731 Conservative Party: Clapham association 4pp *British L of Polit and Econ Science*

29732 British Association for Early Childhood Education 3pp *British L of Polit and Econ Science*

29733 Sir Robert Clayton, banker: business and family papers 48pp *British L of Polit and Econ Science*

29734 William John Braithwaite, civil servant: papers rel to the National Insurance Act 13pp *British L of Polit and Econ Science*

29735 Sir Gerald Reid Barry, journalist: corresp and papers 10pp *British L of Polit and Econ Science*

29736 Russell family, Dukes of Bedford: household accounts 12pp *British L of Polit and Econ Science*

29737 Henry Solly: collection rel to conditions of working classes 54pp *British L of Polit and Econ Science*

29738 Huddersfield: Gledholt Methodist Church 1p *Kirklees District Archives*

29739 Heckmondwike Carpets Ltd, Dewsbury 5pp *Kirklees District Archives*

29740 Batley Christmas Dole and Charity Organisation 1p *Kirklees District Archives*

29741 Newsome South Methodist Church 1p *Kirklees District Archives*

29742 J Blackburn & Co Ltd, worsted mfrs, Batley 6pp *Kirklees District Archives*

29743 John Murgatroyd, master of Slaithwaite Free School: diaries and notebooks 4pp *Kirklees District Archives*

29744 Lister Kaye family, baronets, of Denby Grange: deeds and misc papers 6pp *Kirklees District Archives*

29745 Huddersfield and District Public Health Union 1p *Kirklees District Archives*

29746 Cleckheaton township 1p *Kirklees District Archives*

29747 Denby Dale Methodist Circuit 1p *Kirklees District Archives*

29748 Major-General Charles Barnett: order and letter books 24pp *National Army Mus*

29749 William Hughes of Tynyffordd: corresp and papers 73pp *Gwynedd Archives Service, Caernarfon*

29750 Caernarvonshire shipping records 7pp *Gwynedd Archives Service, Caernarfon*

29751 Welsh Water Authority, Caerns: records of predecessor bodies 20pp *Gwynedd Archives Service, Caernarfon*

29752 David Williams, solicitor, Caernarfon: deeds and papers 18pp *Gwynedd Archives Service, Caernarfon*

29753 Richard Bowton & Co Ltd, slate merchants, Portmadoc 73pp *Gwynedd Archives Service, Caernarfon*

29754 Yale & Hardcastle, surveyors and estate agents, Caernarfon 128pp *Gwynedd Archives Service, Caernarfon*

29755 University College of North Wales, Bangor: Students Union 102pp *Gwynedd Archives Service, Caernarfon*

29756 Edwin J Foy & Sons Ltd, ironmongers and furniture dealers, Minehead 1p *Somerset RO*

29757 Wells: Mendip Hospital 8pp *Somerset RO*

29758 North Petherton: Sir Thomas Wroth Charity 2pp *Somerset RO*

29759 Ernst family of Westcombe: corresp and papers 7pp *Somerset RO*

29760 Canon George E Macaulay Bennett: travel diaries 2pp *Somerset RO*

29761 John Walker & Sons Ltd, whisky distillers, London 7pp *Private*

29762 Church of England Central Board of Finance 268pp *Church House Record Centre*

29763 Robert White, rector of Dundonald, co Down: corresp and papers 8pp *Trinity Coll L, Dublin*

29764 Church of England Board for Mission and Unity 171pp *Church House Record Centre*

29765 Wilbraham Fitz-John Trench, professor of English Literature: corresp and papers 12pp *Trinity Coll L, Dublin*

29766 Fitzgerald family, Dukes of Leinster: Irish deeds and papers 24pp *Trinity Coll L, Dublin*

29767 Church of England Sunday School Institute 4pp *Church House Record Centre*

29768 London: Society of Patrons of the Anniversary of the Charity Schools 2pp *Church House Record Centre*

29769 Sir John Newport, Irish politician and banker: corresp and papers 12pp *Queens Univ L, Belfast*

29770 Ellesmere Port borough 1p *Cheshire RO*

29771 Winwick Hospital 2pp *Cheshire RO*

29772 Broxton petty sessions 2pp *Cheshire RO*

29773 Chester Castle petty sessions 3pp *Cheshire RO*

29774 Cheshire rural deaneries 6pp *Cheshire RO*

29775 Arden family, Barons Alvanley: estate papers 1p *Cheshire RO*

29776 Achille Serre Ltd, dry cleaners, Walthamstow 6pp *Waltham Forest Archives*

29777 Abney Park Cemetery Co, Chingford 8pp *Waltham Forest Archives*

29778 British Xylonite Ltd 10pp *Waltham Forest Archives*

29779 Indian Tea Association 117pp *India Office L*

29780 Harry Verelst, governor of Bengal: corresp and papers 18pp *India Office L*

29781 Sir Francis Edward Younghusband, soldier, diplomat and explorer: corresp and papers 54pp *India Office L*

29782 Wimbledon Society Museum: MS collection 119pp *Wimbledon Soc Mus*

29783 John Clare, poet: literary MSS and collection rel to him[1] 80pp *Peterborough Mus*

29784 Sir Ronald Gough Waterhouse, judge: corresp and papers 4pp *Clwyd RO, Hawarden*

29785 Dorset schools 30pp *Multiple locations*

29786 Lister Institute of Preventive Medicine 63pp *CMAC, Wellcome Inst*

29787 Percy Cyril Claude Garnham, professor of medical proto-zoology: corresp and papers 89pp *CMAC, Wellcome Inst*

29788 RJ Hetherington, physician: papers rel to contraception 17pp *CMAC, Wellcome Inst*

29789 Abortion Law Reform Association 106pp *CMAC, Wellcome Inst*

29790 Lillias Hamilton, physician and warden of Studley College, Warwicks: corresp and papers 7pp *CMAC, Wellcome Inst*

29791 Suffolk schools 22pp *Suffolk RO, Ipswich and Suffolk RO, Bury St Edmunds*

29792 William Gaskoin Stutter, physician, Wickhambrook: papers 8pp *Suffolk RO, Bury St Edmunds*

29793 Philip Rainsford Evans, paediatrician: corresp and papers 8pp *CMAC, Wellcome Inst*

29794 Melanie Klein, psychoanalyst: corresp and papers 21pp *CMAC, Wellcome Inst*

29795 Sir Alexander Haddow, experimental pathologist: diaries, notebooks and corresp 7pp *CMAC, Wellcome Inst*

29796 Walsham-le-Willows charities 6pp *Suffolk RO, Bury St Edmunds*

29797 Brent Eleigh charities 1p *Suffolk RO, Bury St Edmunds*

29798 Bury St Edmunds: Churchgate Street Unitarian Chapel 1p *Suffolk RO, Bury St Edmunds*

---

[1] M Grainger *A descriptive catalogue of the John Clare collection in Peterborough Museum and Art Gallery,* 1973

29799 Sir Ernest Lawrence Kennaway, experimental pathologist: notebooks 2pp *CMAC, Wellcome Inst*

29800 Nayland with Wissington: British Legion Sanatorium 11pp *Suffolk RO, Bury St Edmunds*

29801 Alton: Normandy Street Congregational Chapel 1p *Hants RO*

29802 Fordingbridge Cottage Hospital 1p *Hants RO*

29803 Eastleigh petty sessions 3pp *Hants RO*

29804 Ringwood and Fordingbridge Citizens Advice Bureau 1p *Hants RO*

29805 Titchfield Congregational Church 1p *Hants RO*

29806 Broughton and Bossington Horticultural Society 1p *Hants RO*

29807 Conservative Party: Winchester association 5pp *Hants RO*

29808 Winchester Diocesan Services Mission 5pp *Hants RO*

29809 John Croad, builders and decorators, Fareham 3pp *Hants RO*

29810 Bournemouth Methodist District 1p *Hants RO*

29811 Winchester Young Farmers Club 1p *Hants RO*

29812 Fareham Citizens Advice Bureau 2pp *Hants RO*

29813 Workers Educational Association: Winchester branch 1p *Hants RO*

29814 Winchester and District Society of Arts 1p *Hants RO*

29815 Incorporated Clergy Sustentation Fund 1p *Hants RO*

29816 Winchester Swimming Club 1p *Hants RO*

29817 Frederick Alfred John Emery-Wallis, leader of Hampshire County Council: corresp and papers 4pp *Hants RO*

29818 Hampshire schools 49pp *Hants RO*

29819 North Wales Chronicle Co Ltd, Bangor 59pp *Gwynedd Archives Service, Caernarfon*

29820 Gwenlyn Evans, printers, Caernarfon 4pp *Gwynedd Archives Service, Caernarfon*

29821 Henry Ballantyne & Sons Ltd, tweed mfrs, Walkerburn, Peeblesshire 11pp *Edinburgh Univ L*

29822 Schoolmistresses and Governesses Benevolent Institution 34pp *Private*

29823 Duff family, baronets, of Vaynol; corresp and papers incl those of Assheton-Smith family 1396pp *Gwynedd Archives Service, Caernarfon*

29824 Evan R Davies & Davies, solicitors, Pwllheli: deeds 58pp *Gwynedd Archives Service, Caernarfon*

29825 Nanney family of Gwynfryn, Caerns, and Cefndauddwr, Merioneth: estate papers 10pp *Gwynedd Archives Service, Caernarfon*

29826 Kenrick Evans, writer on Caernarfon history: corresp and papers 63pp *Gwynedd Archives Service, Caernarfon*

29827 Rees family of Plas Brereton: corresp and papers 152pp *Gwynedd Archives Service, Caernarfon*

29828 Breese, Jones & Casson, solicitors, Portmadoc: misc papers 8pp *Gwynedd Archives Service, Caernarfon*

29829 Ellis family of Glasfryn, Caerns: corresp and papers 43pp *Private*

29830 Chester Ladies Hockey Club 3pp *Chester City RO*

29831 Upton by Chester Golf Club 1p *Chester City RO*

29832 Susanna Leveson-Gower, Marchioness of Stafford: letters to her daughter, Charlotte, Duchess of Beaufort 25pp *Birmingham Univ L*

29833 Sevenoaks Rural District Council 13pp *Kent AO and Kent AO, Sevenoaks*

29834 Sevenoaks: Lady Boswell's Charity 16pp *Kent AO*

29835 Sevenoaks Methodist Circuit 11pp *Kent AO*

29836 CJ Hudson Ltd, flour mills, Ramsgate 6pp *Kent AO, Ramsgate*

29837 Hooker Brothers, printers and stationers, Westerham 9pp *Kent AO, Sevenoaks*

29838 Ceiriog Valley Woollen Mills, Glynceiriog, Denbighs 3pp *Univ Coll of N Wales, Bangor*

29839 Birmingham Canal Navigations 4pp *Birmingham Reference L*

29840 EH James Ltd, wine and spirit merchants, Birmingham 7pp *Birmingham Reference L*

29841 Hatwell Pritchett & Co, solicitors, Birmingham: clients papers 4pp *Birmingham Reference L*

29842 JW Bond & Co, horseshoe and metal mfrs, Birmingham 1p *Birmingham Reference L*

29843 Price, Atkins and Price, solicitors, Birmingham: deeds 20pp *Birmingham Reference L*

29844 Foster, Pettitt & Simcox, solicitors, Birmingham: deeds 23pp *Birmingham Reference L*

29845 G&J Zair, whip makers, Birmingham 4pp *Birmingham Reference L*

29846 Cornelius and Ebenezer Robins and Robert Gillam of Birmingham: business and estate papers 24pp *Birmingham Reference L*

29847 Birmingham Reference Library: misc accessions 432pp *Birmingham Reference L*

29848 Southwark board of guardians 14pp *Greater London RO*

29849 George Matlock Brockman Burt 'Michael Burt', author: papers 5pp *W Sussex RO*

29850 Arundel Clerical Association 1p *W Sussex RO*

29851 Chichester Ballet Club 2pp *W Sussex RO*

29852 Newnham family of Ardingly: papers 16pp *W Sussex RO*

29853 John Talbott, steward to 3rd Viscount Montague: corresp and misc papers 3pp *W Sussex RO*

29854 Captain George Yule, RN: corresp and diaries 5pp *Private*

29855 Crawley and District Community Association 2pp *W Sussex RO*

29856 Robert Horne Penney, ship-owner and manager, Southwick 1p *W Sussex RO*

29857 Mid-Sussex Ploughing and Agricultural Association 1p *W Sussex RO*

29858 Lucas family of Warnham Court: corresp and papers 20pp *W Sussex RO*

29859 Walker Brothers Ltd, iron and steel mfrs, Walsall 5pp *Walsall Archives*

29860 Pimms Ltd, beverage mfrs, London 17pp *Private*

29861 Peckham Building Society 5pp *Private*

29862 Godalming Careers Office 1p *Surrey RO, Kingston*

29863 Surrey schools 12pp *Surrey RO, Kingston*

29864 Hay family, Marquesses of Tweeddale: deeds and estate papers 526pp *Scottish RO*

29865 Lawson family, Barons Burnham: deeds and papers 239pp *Private*

29866 Howell Arthur Gwynne, journalist: First World War corresp 26pp *Imperial War Mus*

29867 Hertfordshire Baptist chapels 6pp *Herts RO*

29868 Hertfordshire County Association of Change Ringers 2pp *Herts RO*

29869 Berkhamsted borough 15pp *Herts RO*

29870 Bishops Stortford Urban District Council 8pp *Herts RO*

29871 Stanstead Abbotts: Countess of Huntingdon Connexion Chapel 3pp *Herts RO*

29872 Bagge family, baronets, of Stradsett Hall, Norfolk: family and estate papers 2pp *Private*

29873 Barnwell family of Mileham, Norfolk: deeds and papers 2pp *Private*

29874 Hugh Reginald Haweis, author and preacher: personal and family corresp and papers 128pp *British Columbia Univ L, Canada*

29875 William Russell, merchant and reformer: corresp and papers 56pp *Various locations*

29876 Labour Party: Windsor division 2pp *Berks RO*

29877 Waltham St Lawrence Band 3pp *Berks RO*

29878 Twyford United Reformed Church 10pp *Berks RO*

29879 Byng family, Viscounts Torrington: corresp and papers 6pp *Private*

29880 George Grote, historian, and Harriet Grote, biographer: diaries and corresp 4pp *Univ Coll London*

29881 Mervyn Peake, author and artist: literary MSS and misc corresp 2pp *Univ Coll London*

29882 Arnold Bennett, author: corresp and papers rel to his estate 4pp *Univ Coll London*

29883 Greasbrough Wesleyan Methodist Church 1p *Rotherham Central L*

29884 Trotter of The Bush, Midlothian: family and estate papers 57pp *Private*

29985 Hope family, Marquesses of Linlithgow: estate papers 28pp *Private*

29886 Forth Tugs Ltd, towage contractors, Grangemouth 5pp *Glasgow Univ Archives*

29887 Willow Bank Bowling Club, Glasgow 5pp *Private*

29888 Wallsend borough petty sessions 3pp *Tyne and Wear Archives Dept*

29889 Norwich: Chapel-in-the-Field Congregational Church 14pp *Norfolk RO*

29890 Norwich: Unthank Road Baptist Church 1p *Norfolk RO*

29891 Goodchild family of Great Yeldham Hall: family and estate papers 12pp *Essex RO*

29892 Essex Rural Community Council 1pp *Essex RO*

29893 Danbury Society 5pp *Essex RO*

29894 Charles Bradlaugh, freethinker and politician: personal and family corresp and papers[1] 184pp *Bishopsgate Inst, London*

29895 Association of Assistant Mistresses 29pp *Warwick Univ L*

29896 James Abercromby, 1st Baron Dunfermline: political and family corresp and papers 4pp *National L of Scotland*

29897 Colonial Bank, Trinidad[2] 77pp *Univ of W Indies, St Augustine, Trinidad*

29898 Sir Robert William Duff, 4th Bt, politician and colonial governor: corresp and papers 4pp *Scottish RO*

29899 Baskerville family of Richardson, Winterbourne Bassett: deeds and papers 12pp *Wilts RO*

29900 Trowbridge Tabernacle Church 11pp *Wilts RO*

29901 Vulcan Foundry Ltd, locomotive engineers, Newton-le-Willows 77pp *National Mus on Merseyside*

29902 Rodney Robert Porter, biochemist: corresp and papers 64pp *Bodleian L, Oxford*

29903 Sloane Stanley of Paultons: family and estate papers 23pp *Hants RO*

29904 London: British Hospital for Mothers and Babies 56pp *Greater London RO*

29905 Hodbarrow Mining Co Ltd, iron ore proprietors, Millom 23pp *Cumbria RO, Barrow in Furness*

29906 Kensington: St Mary Abbots Hospital 37pp *Greater London RO*

29907 Erpingham Methodist Church 1p *Norfolk RO*

29908 Herefordshire schools 1p *Heref and Worc RO, Hereford*

29909 Marham Poors Allotment Trustees 2pp *Norfolk RO*

29910 Norwich: Scots Society of St Andrew 2pp *Norfolk RO*

29911 West Norfolk Clerical Society 2pp *Norfolk RO*

29912 Norfolk schools 6pp *Norfolk RO*

29913 Dyfed Archives, Carmarthenshire Record Office: misc accessions 10pp *Dyfed Archives, Carmarthen*

29914 Norwich Council of Churches 1p *Norfolk RO*

29915 Norwich Freemasons: Naval and Military Lodge 1p *Norfolk RO*

29916 Jones family of Bryntirion: deeds 14pp *Gwynedd Archives Service, Caernarfon*

29917 Philip Constable Ellis, rector of Llanfairfechan: Caerns deeds 20pp *Gwynedd Archives Service, Caernarfon*

29918 Hughes (formerly Thomas) family of Coed Helen: deeds and estate papers 41pp *Gwynedd Archives Service, Caernarfon*

29919 John Jones, sea captain, Portmadoc: family corresp and papers 25pp *Gwynedd Archives Service, Caernarfon*

29920 Bangor diocese: misc papers 14pp *Gwynedd Archives Service, Caernarfon*

29921 Williams family of Abererch, Caerns: papers 28pp *Gwynedd Archives Service, Caernarfon*

29922 Llanberis: papers rel to chapel buildings 100pp *Gwynedd Archives Service, Caernarfon*

29923 Caernarfon: Calvinistic Methodist Bookroom collection 33pp *Gwynedd Archives Service, Caernarfon*

[1] E Royle *The Bradlaugh Papers. A descriptive index,* 1975
[2] MD Rouse-Jones *The Colonial Bank Correspondence 1837–1885,* 1986

29924 Ioan Glynne, solicitor, Bangor: family deeds and papers 134pp *Gwynedd Archives Service, Caernarfon*

29925 Hughes family, farmers, Clynnog: papers 47pp *Gwynedd Archives Service, Caernarfon*

29926 Bangor Methodist Circuit 78pp *Gwynedd Archives Service, Caernarfon*

29927 Llandudno Junction: Capel Coffa Welsh Independent Chapel 17pp *Gwynedd Archives Service, Caernarfon*

29928 Charity Commission: Caerns charities accounts 89pp *Gwynedd Archives Service, Caernarfon*

29929 Gordon H Richards, slate merchant, Caernarfon 15pp *Gwynedd Archives Service, Caernarfon*

29930 Hurst Hill Methodist Church 1p *Wolverhampton Central L*

29931 George Coggins, solicitor, Deddington 1p *Oxon RO*

29932 Christopher Muller, commission agent, London 3pp *Greater London RO*

29933 Seagers Ltd, mechanical engineers, Dartford 7pp *Kent AO*

29934 Southampton Free Church Federal Council 2pp *Southampton City RO*

29935 Charity Commission: Southampton charities accounts 3pp *Southampton City RO*

★29936 Talbot family, Barons Talbot de Malahide: family and estate papers 58pp *Bodleian L, Oxford*

29937 Ragosine Oil Co Ltd, London 23pp *Warwick Univ L*

29938 Baker-Gabb family of Abergavenny, Mon: family and estate papers 304pp *National L of Wales*

29939 Newcastle Regional Hospital Board 39pp *Tyne and Wear Archives Dept*

29940 Gateshead Area Health Authority 1p *Tyne and Wear Archives Dept*

29941 Northumberland schools 1p *Tyne and Wear Archives Dept*

29942 Gateshead: Dunston Hill Hospital 3pp *Tyne and Wear Archives Dept*

29943 George Darling, Baron Darling: corresp and papers 3pp *Sheffield Central L*

29944 Climbers Club 16pp *Gwynedd Archives Service, Caernarfon*

29945 Caernarvonshire Insurance Committee 2pp *Gwynedd Archives Service, Caernarfon*

29946 Caernarvonshire lieutenancy 7pp *Gwynedd Archives Service, Caernarfon*

29947 National Savings Movement: Caerns committees 6pp *Gwynedd Archives Service, Caernarfon*

29948 Blades, dispensing chemists, Llandudno 5pp *Gwynedd Archives Service, Caernarfon*

29949 Inigo Jones Ltd, slate mfrs, Groeslon 1p *Gwynedd Archives Service, Caernarfon*

29950 Anwyl Roberts family: Caerns, Denbighs and Merioneth deeds and papers 14pp *Gwynedd Archives Service, Caernarfon*

29951 Williams family of Bron y Fuches, Dinorwic: family and estate papers 25pp *Gwynedd Archives Service, Caernarfon*

29952 Hughes family of Edern: corresp and papers 79pp *Gwynedd Archives Service, Caernarfon*

29953 Kinross House, Kinross-shire: papers (Bruce and Graham families) 183pp *Scottish RO and Private*

29954 Shairp of Houstoun, W Lothian: family and estate papers 367pp *Scottish RO*

29955 William McKnight Docharty, mountaineer: diaries 1p *National L of Scotland*

29956 Archibald Richard Burdon Haldane, writer: corresp and notes 1p *National L of Scotland*

29957 Lindsay, Jamieson & Haldane, accountants, Edinburgh 1p *National L of Scotland*

29958 Ruthven Campbell Todd, writer and poet: corresp and papers 1p *National L of Scotland*

29959 Francis M Collinson, composer: corresp and papers mainly rel to Scots folk music 13pp *National L of Scotland*

29960 Sir Joseph Noel Paton, artist: corresp and misc papers 3pp *National L of Scotland*

29961 Cameron family, baronets, of Fassifern, Argyllshire: family and estate papers 7pp *National L of Scotland*

29962 William Stevenson, missionary to India: corresp and misc papers 2pp *National L of Scotland*

29963 Lt-General Sir David Henderson: First World War corresp 1p *National L of Scotland*

29964 Gairm Publications, Glasgow 4pp *National L of Scotland*

29965 Saltoun Church, E Lothian: MS collection 4pp *National L of Scotland*

29966 William Johnstone, artist: corresp 1p *National L of Scotland*

29967 Griggs family of Wigwell Grange: deeds and papers 17pp *Derbys RO*

29968 Derby and South Derbyshire Magistrates Court: records of predecessor authorities 18pp *Derbys RO*

29969 Enfield and District Carnation Society 11pp *Greater London RO*

29970 Battersea General Hospital 24pp *Greater London RO*

29971 Trinity House, South Shields 1p *Tyne and Wear Archives Dept*

29972 John Bodvan Anwyl, Celtic scholar: corresp and sermons 246pp *National L of Wales*

29973 Bagot family, Barons Bagot: Denbighs deeds 340pp *National L of Wales*

29974 Abbey National Building Society 22pp *Private*

29975 Herbert family, Earls of Pembroke: Irish estate papers 160pp *PRO of Ireland*

29976 Wyndham family, Barons Leconfield: Irish estate papers 13pp *PRO of Ireland*

29977 Barmouth Harbour Trust, Merioneth 61pp *National L of Wales*

29978 Phillipps of Longworth, Herefs: misc family and estate papers 21pp *National L of Wales*

29979 Wynne family of Bodewryd, Anglesey: family and estate papers 210pp *National L of Wales*

29980 Aberystwyth Corn and General Market Co 89pp *National L of Wales*

29981 Breconshire Quarter Sessions 37pp *National L of Wales*

29982 Association of Welsh Local Authorities 17pp *National L of Wales*

29983 Aberystwyth borough 8pp *National L of Wales*

29984 Charles Tennyson D'Eyncourt MP: corresp and papers rel to Lambeth elections 3pp *Lambeth Archives Dept*

29985 Dronsfield Brothers Ltd, textile machinery mfrs, Oldham 3pp *Oldham Local Interest Centre*

29986 Werneth Ring Mills Ltd, cotton spinners, Oldham 5pp *Oldham Local Interest Centre*

29987 A&A Crompton & Co Ltd, cotton spinners and weavers, East Crompton 3pp *Oldham Local Interest Centre*

29988 JF&C Kenworthy Ltd, woollen mfrs, Uppermill, Yorks 3pp *Oldham Local Interest Centre*

29989 J Chadwick & Co Ltd, dyers and calico printers, Oldham 5pp *Oldham Local Interest Centre*

29990 Scully family of Kilfeacle, co Tipperary: corresp and papers 22pp *National L of Ireland*

29991 Christchurch and Bournemouth board of guardians 11pp *Dorset RO*

29992 Archibald Henry Macdonald Sinclair, 1st Viscount Thurso: corresp and papers 131pp *Churchill Coll, Cambridge*

29993 Christopher Hinton, Baron Hinton of Bankside: misc papers 12pp *Churchill Coll, Cambridge*

29994 George Ronald Lewin, military historian: corresp and papers 23pp *Churchill Coll, Cambridge*

29995 John Churchill, 1st Duke of Marlborough: corresp 7pp *Churchill Coll, Cambridge*

29996 Robert and Sybil Hutton: papers rel to European refugees 7pp *Churchill Coll, Cambridge*

29997 James Hope, United Irishman: misc papers 4pp *Trinity Coll L, Dublin*

29998 Samuel Greg & Co, cotton spinners and doublers, Styal, Cheshire 16pp *Manchester Central L and Private*

29999 Acheson family, Earls of Gosford: family and estate papers 392pp *PRO of N Ireland*

30000 Talbot of Margam and Penrice, Glamorgan: family and estate papers 2278pp *National L of Wales*

30001 O'Connell family of Derrynane, co Kerry: corresp and papers 440pp *Univ Coll, Dublin*

30002 Abdullah Abdurahman, South African politician: corresp and papers rel to African People's Organisation 22pp *Private*

30003 Zachariah Keodirelang Matthews, South African politician: corresp and papers 11pp *Private*

30004 Holland House Electrical Co Ltd, Glasgow 3pp *Private*

30005 Alexander Thomson, Advocate and Free Church benefactor: travel journal and misc papers 5pp *Aberdeen Univ L*

30006 Alexander Dyce Davidson, Free church minister: lectures and sermons 5pp *Aberdeen Univ L*

30007 Aberdeen Trawl Owners & Traders Engineering Co Ltd 4pp *Aberdeen Univ L*

30008 John Walker & Sons Ltd, whisky distillers, Kilmarnock, Ayrshire 27pp *Private*

30009 Child-Villiers family, Earls of Jersey: Glamorgan deeds 114pp *National L of Wales*

30010 Newcastle upon Tyne: Portland Park Bowling Green Club 3pp *Tyne and Wear Archives Dept*

30011 Wallsend and Willington Quay Moral Welfare Association 3pp *Tyne and Wear Archives Dept*

30012 West Denton: John Knox United Reformed Church 4pp *Tyne and Wear Archives Dept*

30013 Newcastle upon Tyne: St George's United Reformed Church, High Heaton 18pp *Tyne and Wear Archives Dept*

30014 Blaydon petty sessions 2pp *Tyne and Wear Archives Dept*

30015 Caernarvon Harbour Trust 206pp *Private*

30016 Caernarfon borough 160pp *Gwynedd Archives Service, Caernarfon*

30017 Caernarfon Methodist Circuit 190pp *Gwynedd Archives Service, Caernarfon*

30018 Ormskirk petty sessions 7pp *Lancs RO*

30019 Carter, Vincent & Co, solicitors, Bangor: deeds and papers (various counties) 109pp *Gwynedd Archives Service, Caernarfon*

30020 Solomon Andrews & Son Ltd, property developers and retailers, Cardiff: papers mainly rel to North Wales 859pp *Gwynedd Archives Service, Caernarfon*

30021 Lloyd family, baronets, of Bronwydd, Cards: barony of Kemes, Pembs, papers 103pp *National L of Wales*

30022 Nevill family, Marquesses of Abergavenny: Mon and Herefs deeds and estate papers 304pp *National L of Wales*

30023 Vesey family, Viscounts de Vesci: family and estate papers 171pp *Private*

30024 Fitzalan-Howard family, Dukes of Norfolk: Norfolk and Suffolk estate papers 2pp *Norfolk RO*

30025 Henry William Massingham, journalist: corresp 16pp *Norfolk RO*

30026 Wyche family of Hockwold: family and estate papers 11pp *Norfolk RO*

30027 Arthur Campling, genealogist: Norfolk collections 12pp *Norfolk RO*

30028 William Burgess Hunt Chandler, clergyman: Norfolk local history collections 16pp *Norfolk RO*

30029 Edward Meyrick Goulburn, dean of Norwich: corresp 1p *Norfolk RO*

30030 Ringer family of Forncett: family and estate papers 15pp *Norfolk RO*

30031 Tyssen-Amherst (afterwards Cecil) family, Barons Amherst of Hackney: family and Norfolk estate papers 84pp *Norfolk RO*

30032 General Sir Alan Gordon Cunningham: corresp and papers 7pp *National Army Mus*

30033 Electrical Association for Women: Thames Valley branch 2pp *Surrey RO, Kingston*

30034 Whitton Methodist Church 1p *Surrey RO, Kingston*

30035 Barnes Baptist Church 7pp *Surrey RO, Kingston*

30036 Lloyd of Aston, Shopshire: family and estate papers 2814pp *National L of Wales*

30037 Preston borough petty sessions 30pp *Lancs RO*

30038 Westhoughton: Sacred Heart Roman Catholic Church 2pp *Lancs RO*

30039 Lancashire schools 12pp *Lancs RO*

30040 Bernard Bolingbroke Woodward, librarian and author: misc corresp and papers 5pp *Norfolk RO*

30041 Boileau family, baronets, of Tacolnestone: deeds and papers 8pp *Norfolk RO*

30042 Norwich: Rosary Cemetery 2pp *Norfolk RO*

30043 Hollway-Calthrop family of Stanhoe: deeds and papers 7pp *Norfolk RO*

30044 Henley family of Winsham, Somerset: Sandringham deeds 4pp *Norfolk RO*

30045 Gurdon family, Barons Cranworth: Norfolk deeds and estate papers 62pp *Norfolk RO*

30046 Cooper family of North Walsham: family and estate papers 10pp *Norfolk RO*

30047 Brett family, Viscounts Esher: corresp 4pp *Liverpool Univ L*

30048 Kemp family, baronets, of Gissing: misc deeds and estate papers 4pp *Norfolk RO*

30049 Bond-Cabell of Cromer: family and estate papers 22pp *Norfolk RO*

30050 William Heveningham, regicide: personal and estate corresp and papers 9pp *Norfolk RO*

30051 Charles Frobisher, highway engineer and surveyor: corresp and papers 2pp *Norfolk RO*

30052 Jonathan Matchett, newspaper proprietor: Norfolk collections 1p *Norfolk RO*

30053 John and Randall Wells, saddlers, North Elmham 2pp *Norfolk RO*

30054 Norwich: St Peters Park Lane Methodist Church 1p *Norfolk RO*

30055 Loddon and Clavering petty sessions 1p *Norfolk RO*

30056 Sparham rural deanery 1p *Norfolk RO*

30057 Norwich: Countess of Huntingdon Connexion Tabernacle 1p *Norfolk RO*

30058 Campden petty sessions 1p *Glos RO*

30059 Northleach petty sessions 1p *Glos RO*

30060 Stow-on-the-Wold petty sessions 1p *Glos RO*

30061 Thornbury petty sessions 1p *Glos RO*

30062 Winchcombe petty sessions 1p *Glos RO*

30063 Gloucestershire schools 200pp *Multiple locations*

30064 Fletchers, gunsmiths and sports equipment dealers, Gloucester 11pp *Glos RO*

30065 James Philip Moore, architect, Gloucester: papers 37pp *Glos RO*

30066 Coalway Recreation Ground Committee 2pp *Glos RO*

30067 Hertfordshire schools 20pp *Herts RO*

30068 Huntingdonshire schools 10pp *Cambs RO, Huntingdon*

30069 HT Gaddum & Co Ltd, silk and man made fibre yarn merchants, Macclesfield 9pp *Private*

30070 Scottish United Services Museum: military MS collection 10pp *Scottish United Services Mus*

30071 Wilshere family of The Fryth: estate papers 23pp *Herts RO*

30072 Central Brighton Traders Association 3pp *E Sussex RO*

30073 National Federation of Business and Professional Womens Clubs: Eastbourne branch 2pp *E Sussex RO*

30074 Ancient Order of Druids: Lewes Coronation Lodge No 552 4pp *E Sussex RO*

30075 Arthur Tester Ltd, builders, St Leonards 3pp *E Sussex RO*

30076 Beard & Co (Lewes) Ltd, brewers and wine spirit merchants 35pp *E Sussex RO*

30077 Gordon family, Marquesses of Aberdeen and Temair: family and Aberdeenshire estate papers 232pp *Scottish RO*

30078 Rose family of Montcoffer, Banffshire: family and estate papers 48pp *Scottish RO*

30079 Steuart of Dalguise, Perthshire: family and estate papers 242pp *Scottish RO*

30080 Cunningham family, Earls of Glencairn: family and estate papers 93pp *Scottish RO*

30081 Warrington: Victoria Park Maternity Home 1p *Cheshire RO*

30082 Warrington Dispensary and Infirmary 3pp *Cheshire RO*

30083 Audlem Public Hall 1p *Cheshire RO*

30084 Cheshire National Health Executive Council 2pp *Cheshire RO*

30085 Tollemache family, Barons Tollemache: deeds and estate papers 27pp *Cheshire RO*

30086 Erpingham Lodge estate: deeds 5pp *Norfolk RO*

30087 Macclesfield: Parkside Hospital 6pp *Cheshire RO*

30088 A & JE Fletcher, solicitors, Northwich 31pp *Cheshire RO*

30089 Simeon's Trustees 20pp *Cambridge Univ L*

30090 Thornton family of Clapham, Surrey: corresp and papers 7pp *Cambridge Univ L*

30091 Silchester Methodist Circuit 13pp *Hants RO*

30092 Spreyton board of guardians 15pp *Devon RO*

30093 CR Claridge & Sons Ltd, timber merchants and motor vehicle dealers, Exeter and Heythrop, Oxon 2pp *Devon RO*

30094 Mills Bros, ironmongers, Crediton 2pp *Devon RO*

30095 Devon Schools 12pp *Devon RO*

30096 Newton Abbot Rural District Council 1p *Devon RO*

30097 South Molton: Beech House 2pp *Devon RO*

30098 Ashburton Society of Friends 1p *Devon RO*

30099 Staines and District Citizens Advice Bureau 22pp *Greater London RO*

30100 Queen Adelaide's Fund 8pp *Greater London RO*

30101 Stewart-Mackenzie of Seaforth, Inverness-shire and Ross and Cromarty: family and estate papers 295pp *Scottish RO*

30102 Barclay Allardice family of Allardice, Kincardineshire: family and estate papers 72pp *Scottish RO*

30103 John Macgregor, antiquary: Scottish collections 35pp *Scottish RO*

30104 Berisfords plc, ribbon mfrs, Congleton, Cheshire 7pp *Private*

30105 Corbyn, Stacey & Co, manufacturing chemists, London 3pp *Beds RO*

30106 Biggleswade Clergy Association 3pp *Beds RO*

30107 Leighton Buzzard Methodist Circuit 11pp *Beds RO*

30108 Dunstable: Jane Cart's Trust 14pp *Beds RO*

30109 Bedford: Riverside Lawn Tennis Club 3pp *Beds RO*

30110 Frederick Thomas Cox, printer, stationer and newsagent, Potton 43pp *Beds RO*

30111 Ashburnham family, Earls of Ashburnham: Beds estate papers 43pp *Beds RO*

30112 Cust family, Earls Brownlow: Beds family and estate papers 110pp *Beds RO*

30113 Harris family of Leighton Buzzard: corresp and misc papers 10pp *Beds RO*

30114 Whitbread of Southill: family and estate papers 625pp *Beds RO*

30115 Sir Herbert Charles Jones, builder: personal and business papers 22pp *Beds RO*

30116 Polhill of Howbury: family and estate papers 22pp *Beds RO*

30117 Bedford Primitive Methodist Circuit 2pp *Beds RO*

30118 Bedfordshire boy scouts 5pp *Beds RO*

30119 Bedford: St Etheldreda's Childrens Home 2pp *Beds RO*

30120 WJ Trotter & Son, auctioneers, valuers, estate and insurance agents, Macclesfield 8pp *Cheshire RO*

30121 National Maritime Museum: MS collections 1150pp *National Maritime Mus*

30122 Derbyshire schools 4pp *Derbys RO*

30123 Kent schools 4pp *Kent AO*

30124 FJ Pike, shopfitters, Ramsgate 2pp *Kent AO, Ramsgate*

30125 Margate: Lying-in Charity 4pp *Kent AO, Ramsgate*

30126 Courtaulds Spinning, textile and manmade fibre mfrs, Manchester and Oldham 27pp *Private*

30127 Arthur Sanderson & Sons Ltd, mfrs and distributors of wallpaper and furnishing fabrics, Uxbridge, Middx 12pp *Private*

30128 Hugh Richard Lawrie Sheppard, vicar of St Martin-in-the-Fields: personal and family corresp and papers 8pp *Private*

30129 W & T Avery Ltd, weighing machine mfrs, Smethwick 4pp *Private*

30130 British Association for the Advancement of Science 88pp *Bodleian L, Oxford*

30131 Waterloo Mills Cake and Warehousing Co Ltd, Kingston upon Hull 7pp *Hull City RO*

30132 Samuel Greg & Co, cotton spinners and doublers, Styal 73pp *Manchester Central L*

30133 Kent Archives Office, Sevenoaks: misc accessions *Kent AO, Sevenoaks*

30134 Gateshead: Bensham Road Methodist Chapel 2pp *Tyne and Wear Archives Dept*

30135 Lemington: Bells Close Methodist Church 3pp *Tyne and Wear Archives Dept*

30136 Raine's Schools Foundation 68pp *Greater London RO*

30137 Liverpool Ear, Nose and Throat Infirmary 7pp *Liverpool RO*

30138 Liverpool: David Lewis Northern Hospital 13pp *Liverpool RO*

30139 Liverpool: Womens Hospital, Catherine Street 34pp *Liverpool RO*

30140 Molyneux family, Earls of Sefton: diaries and papers 34pp *Liverpool RO*

30141 Fire Salvage Association of Liverpool 38pp *Liverpool RO*

30142 William Rathbone MP: letters from Florence Nightingale 16pp *Liverpool RO*

30143 Liverpool Area Health Authority 41pp *Liverpool RO*

30144 Cadbury Ltd, confectionery mfrs, Birmingham 20pp *Birmingham Univ L*

30145 West Essex Permanent Building Society, Chelmsford 4pp *Essex RO*

30146 Epping Rural District Council 1p *Essex RO*

30147 Castle Point District Council 8pp *Essex RO, Southend*

30148 Institute of Public Relations 93pp *History of Advertising Trust*

30149 British Direct Marketing Association 32pp *History of Advertising Trust*

30150 Association of Independent Radio Contractors Ltd 160pp *History of Advertising Trust*

30151 Victoria and Albert Museum, Department of Textiles: pattern books and textile collections 20pp *Victoria & Albert Mus, Dept of Textiles*

30152 John Augustus Noel Longley, physician, Bristol 14pp *Bristol RO*

30153 Stoke Park Hospital, Stapleton 14pp *Bristol RO*

30154 Bristol: Oakfield Road Unitarian Church 1p *Bristol RO*

30155 Bristol: Southmead Health Authority 6pp *Bristol RO*

30156 Avonmouth Congregational Church 4pp *Bristol RO*

30157 Bristol Guild of the Handicapped 6pp *Bristol RO*

30158 Bristol: Russell Town Congregational Church 5pp *Bristol RO*

30159 Basire Bros & Taylor, sheet metal workers, Bristol 3pp *Bristol RO*

30160 Bristol: Clifton Down Congregational Church 10pp *Bristol RO*

30161 Keynsham: Ebenezer Baptist Church 7pp *Bristol RO*

30162 Frederick George Webb, Bristol: local history papers 23pp *Bristol RO*

30163 Rust family of Fishponds, Bristol: family papers 4pp *Bristol RO*

30164 Philip Leek (Bristol) Ltd, marble and granite merchants 3pp *Bristol RO*

30165 Smith family of Long Ashton: corresp 4pp *Bristol RO*

30166 Sir John Hare, floor cloth mfr, Bristol: corresp and election papers 3pp *Bristol RO*

30167 London: Salters Company 49pp *Private*

30168 Lucas Birch, confectioner and caterer, London 2pp *Guildhall L, London and Mus of London*

30169 Charles Hammond & Son, stockbrokers, London 3pp *Guildhall L, London*

30170 William Cecil, 1st Baron Burghley: letters to Peter Osborne rel to foreign exchange 5pp *Guildhall L, London*

30171 Charles, William and Wentworth Gray, N America merchants, London 5pp *Guildhall L, London*

30172 Anthony Gibbs & Sons Ltd, merchants and bankers, London 79pp *Guildhall L, London*

30173 Royal Insurance plc: records of predecessor companies 38pp *Guildhall L, London*

30174 Birch & Gaydon Ltd, watch, clock and chronometer mfrs, London 5pp *Guildhall L, London*

30175 Davis & Soper Ltd, African and Middle and Far Eastern export merchants, London 2pp *Guildhall L, London*

30176 Gresham House Estate Co Ltd, London 9pp *Guildhall L, London*

30177 Lincolnshire schools 50pp *Lincs AO*

30178 Greater London schools 200pp *Multiple locations*

30179 Charles Frodsham & Co Ltd, watch, clock and chronometer mfrs, London 3pp *Guildhall L, London*

30180 Parkinson & Frodsham, watch, clock and chronometer mfrs, London 4pp *Guildhall L, London*

30181 John Richards and John Rooke, Spanish merchants, London 2pp *Guildhall L, London*

30182 Scottish & Mercantile Investment Co Ltd, London 4pp *Guildhall L, London*

30183 Sir John Charles Walton, Indian civil servant: corresp and papers 6pp *India Office L*

30184 David Symington, Indian civil servant and author: misc corresp and papers 3pp *India Office L*

30185 Sir Theodore Emanuel Gugenheim Gregory, economist: corresp and papers as economic adviser to the government of India 4pp *India Office L*

30186 Sir John McNeill, diplomat: corresp and papers mainly rel to Persia 3pp *India Office L*

30187 Boswell of Balmuto, Fife: family and estate papers 38pp *Scottish RO*

30188 Sir John Clague, Indian civil servant: corresp and papers rel to Burma 7pp *India Office L*

30189 Sir Frederick Blackmore Arnold, Indian civil servant: corresp and papers rel to Burma 4pp *India Office L*

30190 Sir Herbert John Maynard, Indian civil servant: corresp and papers 9pp *India Office L*

30191 Heathcote-Drummond-Willoughby family, Earls of Ancaster: Gwydir estate papers 126pp *Gwynedd Archives Service, Caernarfon*

30192 Edward Hall, antiquary: MS collection 3pp *Wigan RO*

30193 J & R Willmott Ltd, silk throwsters, Sherborne 2pp *Dorset RO*

30194 Fox-Strangways family, Earls of Ilchester: family and estate papers 190pp *Dorset RO*

30195 Robert Battersby & Sons, woollen mfrs, Bury 6pp *Bury Archives*

30196 Thomas Robinson & Co Ltd, dyers and bleachers, Ramsbottom 3pp *Bury Archives*

30197 Joshua Hoyle & Sons Ltd, cotton spinners, Bacup 7pp *Bury Archives*

30198 Advertising Creative Circle 30pp *History of Advertising Trust*

30199 Henrietta Downe (née Thornshill) diaries 125pp *Lambeth Archives Dept*

30200 Gordon family of Cairness and Buthlaw, Aberdeenshire: deeds and papers 27pp *Scottish RO*

30201 North Eastern Group of Flour Millers 8pp *Hull City RO*

30202 Macclesfield Silk Museum: misc accessions *Macclesfield Silk Mus, Cheshire*

30203 Cartwright & Sheldon Ltd, silk mfrs, Macclesfield 38pp *Macclesfield Silk Mus, Cheshire*

30204 J Godwin & Sons, textile designers and card cutters, Manchester and Macclesfield 2pp *Macclesfield Silk Mus, Cheshire*

30205 AJ Worthington & Co (Leek) Ltd, sewing silk and braid mfrs 1p *Macclesfield Silk Mus, Cheshire*

30206 Josiah Smale & Sons Ltd, silk mfrs, Macclesfield 1p *Macclesfield Silk Mus, Cheshire*

★30207 Rothamsted Experimental Station 187pp *Rothamsted Experimental Station, Harpenden, Herts*

30208 Dunmow borough 6pp *Essex RO*

30209 Basildon Citizens Advice Bureau 7pp *Essex RO*

30210 Harlow petty sessions 4pp *Essex RO*

30211 Saffron Walden Countryside Association 3pp *Essex RO*

30212 Harwich borough 5pp *Essex RO, Colchester*

30213 Clacton-on-Sea: Ogilvie School of Recovery 17pp *Essex RO, Colchester*

30214 Dunmow and Braintree Educational Fellowship 4pp *Essex RO*

30215 Leiston United Reformed Church 5pp *Suffolk RO, Ipswich*

30216 Brocklehurst Fabrics Ltd, silk weavers and printers, Macclesfield 25pp *Private*

30217 Forbes family, Lords Forbes: family and estate papers 174pp *Scottish RO*

30218 Elliot family of Clifton Park: Harwood, Roxburghshire, deeds and papers 253pp *Scottish RO*

30219 Ipswich Institute 16pp *Suffolk RO, Ipswich*

30220 Independent Order of Odd-fellows: Wickham Market Lodge 6pp *Suffolk RO, Ipswich*

30221 Newstead family, Suffolk farmers: papers 6pp *Suffolk RO, Ipswich*

30222 Dennington Institute 1p *Suffolk RO, Ipswich*

30223 Eastern Electricity Board: Suffolk undertakings 8pp *Suffolk RO, Ipswich*

30224 Hanwell: St Bernard's Hospital 252pp *Greater London RO*

30225 Abney Park Cemetery Co, Stoke Newington 23pp *Hackney Archives Dept*

30226 Kensington and Chelsea Chamber of Trade and Commerce 3pp *Kensington and Chelsea Central L*

30227 Kensington Foundation Grammar School 6pp *Kensington and Chelsea Central L*

30228 Kerr family, Marquesses of Lothian: corresp and papers, incl Coke, Lamb and Cowper families 251pp *Private*

30229 Oxford University: University College 4pp *Univ Coll, Oxford*

30230 Sidcup Literary and Scientific Society 10pp *Bexley Libraries Dept*

30231 Edgar Joseph Wood, Baptist minister: papers 4pp *Bexley Libraries Dept*

30232 Stickland & Chandler, builders and contractors, Belvedere 2pp *Bexley Libraries Dept*

30233 East Wickham Farm records 2pp *Bexley Libraries Dept*

30234 JS Lloyd & Emyr Williams, solicitors, Wrexham 82pp *Clwyd RO, Ruthin*

30235 Pembroke Urban District Council 137pp *Dublin Public L*

30236 Richard Morris Titmuss, professor of social administration: papers 14pp *British L of Polit and Econ Science*

30237 Womens International League for Peace and Freedom: British section 20pp *British L of Polit and Econ Science*

30238 Sir Joshua Jebb, surveyor-general of convict prisons: corresp and papers 35pp *British L of Polit and Econ Science*

30239 Charles Vickery Drysdale, inventor of scientific instruments and birth control pioneer: papers 9pp *British L of Polit and Econ Science*

30240 League of Nations Union 13pp *British L of Polit and Econ Science*

30241 Ronald William Gordon Mackay, politician: papers 60pp *British L of Polit and Econ Science*

30242 GW Jones and B Donoughue: papers rel to Herbert Morrison 14pp *British L of Polit and Econ Science*

30243 Morris Ginsberg, sociologist: corresp and papers 16pp *British L of Polit and Econ Science*

30244 Labour Party: Merton and Morden constituency 4pp *British L of Polit and Econ Science*

30245 Imre Lakatos, professor of logic: corresp and papers 45pp *British L of Polit and Econ Science*

30246 Violet Rosa Markham (Mrs Carruthers), politician and public servant: corresp and papers 153pp *British L of Polit and Econ Science*

30247 John Desmond Bernal, physicist, and Eileen Bernal: papers rel to peace councils 10pp *British L of Polit and Econ Science*

30248 Sir Henry James Sumner Maine, jurist: notebooks and papers 11pp *British L of Polit and Econ Science*

30249 Labour Party: North Lambeth constituency 4pp *British L of Polit and Econ Science*

30250 Womens Co-operative Guild 7pp *British L of Polit and Econ Science*

30251 Sir William Henry Clark, colonial administrator: misc corresp 3pp *British L of Polit and Econ Science*

30252 Frank Wallis Galton, secretary of the Fabian Society: corresp and papers 8pp *British L of Polit and Econ Science*

30253 National Society of Childrens Nurseries 2pp *British L of Polit and Econ Science*

30254 Reconstruction Committee: womens employment sub-committee 16pp *British L of Polit and Econ Science*

30255 W Rees Jeffreys: papers rel to roads and motor transport 18pp *British L of Polit and Econ Science*

30256 Royal Economic Society 2pp *British L of Polit and Econ Science*

30257 National Institute of Industrial Psychology 27pp *British L of Polit and Econ Science*

30258 George Bernard Shaw: business and financial papers 3pp *British L of Polit and Econ Science*

30259 Richard Henry Tawney, historian: corresp and papers 18pp *British L of Polit and Econ Science*

30260 Southern Water Authority: Otterbourne, Timsbury and Twyford pumping stations 48pp *Hants RO*

30261 White, Brooks & Gilman, solicitors, Winchester: clients papers 73pp *Hants RO*

30262 Morgan Philips Price, MP and journalist: personal and family corresp and papers 11pp *Private*

30263 Barrington & Son, solicitors, Dublin and Limerick: clients papers 35pp *PRO of N Ireland*

30264 JD Bladon: Kirk Ella estate deeds and misc papers 44pp *Hull Univ L*

30265 George Granville Eastwood: papers rel to his biography of Harold Laski 4pp *Hull Univ L*

30266 Hull Subscription Library 7pp *Hull Univ L*

30267 John Cordeaux, ornithologist: corresp and papers 6pp *Hull Univ L*

30268 Richard Garrett Engineering Ltd, Leiston 2pp *Suffolk RO, Ipswich*

30269 Phillips & Piper Ltd, clothing mfrs, Ipswich 4pp *Suffolk RO, Ipswich*

30270 Barker, Son & Isherwood, solicitors, Andover: clients papers 39pp *Hants RO*

30271 Darlington Health Authority 14pp *Durham RO*

30272 Sedgefield: Winterton Hospital 22pp *Durham RO*

30273 Aycliffe Hospital 4pp *Durham RO*

30274 Durham schools 5pp *Durham RO*

30275 Darlington petty sessions 11pp *Durham RO*

30276 Rippon family of Rogerley Hall: deeds and papers 44pp *Durham RO*

30277 Peele and Sadler families of Durham: papers 15pp *Durham RO*

30278 Lynesack and Softley: Bull Piece Charity 5pp *Durham RO*

30279 Hutton Henry Coal Co 8pp *Durham RO*

30280 TW Yellowley, general practitioner, Ryton 3pp *Tyne and Wear Archives Dept*

30281 Keith Lander Best, MP: Ynys Mon constituency corresp and papers 13pp *National L of Wales*

30282 Edward Charles Gurney Boyle, Baron Boyle of Handsworth: corresp and papers 120pp *Brotherton L, Leeds Univ*

30283 Edgar Allison Peers, professor of Spanish: corresp and papers 4pp *Brotherton L, Leeds Univ*

30284 Maidstone: West Borough Congregational Church 2pp *Kent AO*

30285 Maidstone: Grove Road Congregational Church 2pp *Kent AO*

30286 Maidstone: Week Street Chapel 3pp *Kent AO*

30287 Queenborough: Bethel Chapel 2pp *Kent AO*

30288 Maidstone: Rose Yard and King Street Chapels 5pp *Kent AO*

30289 Aldridge and Brownhills petty sessions 6pp *Walsall Archives*

30290 Staffordshire schools 4pp *Staffs RO*

30291 Taylor, Taylor & Hobson Ltd, instrument mfrs, Leicester 3pp *Leics RO*

30292 Winfields Rolling Mills Ltd, Birmingham 7pp *Birmingham Reference L*

30293 Charles Britten, printer and stationer, Birmingham 1p *Birmingham Reference L*

30294 Birmingham: All Saints Mental Hospital, Winson Green 5pp *Birmingham Reference L*

30295 F Davis Ltd, wire rope mfrs, Birmingham 1p *Birmingham Reference L*

30296 Smallwood & Sons Ltd, wine merchants, Birmingham 5pp *Birmingham Reference L*

30297 Guest Keen & Nettlefolds Ltd, ironfounders, Birmingham 2pp *Birmingham Reference L*

30298 Birmingham Penny Bank 1p *Birmingham Reference L*

30299 Sir Richard Threlfall, chemical engineer: corresp and papers 17pp *Birmingham Reference L*

30300 Birmingham Association for the Unmarried Mother and her Child 1p *Birmingham Reference L*

30301 Birmingham and Edgbaston Debating Society 6pp *Birmingham Reference L*

30302 Sutton Coldfield borough petty sessions 1p *Birmingham Reference L*

30303 Midland Arts Club 1p *Birmingham Reference L*

30304 Harborne Cricket Club 1p *Birmingham Reference L*

30305 Richard Cadbury Gibbins & Co, engineers and cranemakers, Birmingham 2pp *Birmingham Reference L*

30306 West Birmingham Hospital Management Committee 2pp *Birmingham Reference L*

30307 Birmingham and Midland Borough Road Club 2pp *Birmingham Reference L*

30308 Lister & Wright Ltd, jewellers and goldsmiths, Birmingham 1p *Birmingham Reference L*

30309 Birmingham Trades Council 1p *Birmingham Reference L*

30310 Birmingham Provident Dispensary: Hockley branch 1p *Birmingham Reference L*

30311 Birmingham Chrysanthemum Society 2pp *Birmingham Reference L*

30312 Catherine Hutton, author: literary MSS and misc papers 10pp *Birmingham Reference L*

30313 Birmingham Pensions Hospital Committee 2pp *Birmingham Reference L*

30314 Saltley: St Peter's College 3pp *Birmingham Reference L*

30315 Kings Norton board of guardians 1p *Birmingham Reference L*

30316 Soho Co-operative Society Ltd, Smethwick 1p *Birmingham Reference L*

30317 Sir Samuel Thomas Evans, MP and judge: corresp and papers 42pp *National L of Wales*

30318 Williams-Wynne of Peniarth: estate and misc family corresp and papers 408pp *National L of Wales*

30319 Chilcot & Williams, corset mfrs, Portsmouth 18pp *Portsmouth City RO*

30320 Bishop Bros (Portsmouth) Ltd, boot and shoe mfrs 16pp *Portsmouth City RO*

30321 Portsea Beneficial Society and Schools 10pp *Portsmouth City RO*

30322 Mills & Son, auctioneers and estate agents, Southsea 15pp *Portsmouth City RO*

30323 David Robert Daniel, local politician and civil servant: corresp and papers 57pp *National L of Wales*

30324 Portsmouth Young Mens Christian Association 1p *Portsmouth City RO*

30325 Rawlings collection incl papers of the Stalkartt family of Southsea 13pp *Portsmouth City RO*

30326 WA Richardson & Co, solicitors, Portsmouth 6pp *Portsmouth City RO*

30327 Sherwell, Wells & Way, solicitors, Southsea 13pp *Portsmouth City RO*

30328 Ridge family of Portsmouth: deeds and papers 13pp *Portsmouth City RO*

30329 Port of Portsmouth Chamber of Commerce 1p *Portsmouth City RO*

30330 Portsmouth and District Street Traders Association 4pp *Portsmouth City RO*

30331 Birmingham board of guardians 6pp *Birmingham Reference L*

30332 Portsmouth Pilot Service 2pp *Portsmouth City RO*

30333 Royal Artillery (Territorial Army): 457 (Wessex) Heavy Anti-Aircraft Regiment 4pp *Portsmouth City RO*

30334 Portsmouth Free Church Council 8pp *Portsmouth City RO*

30335 Portsmouth Family Welfare Association 4pp *Portsmouth City RO*

30336 Fareham Business and Professional Womens Club 2pp *Portsmouth City RO*

30337 W Pink & Sons Ltd, grocers, Portsmouth: family and business papers 8pp *Portsmouth City RO*

30338 AH Barber, ironmongers, Portsmouth 3pp *Portsmouth City RO*

30339 Portsmouth (Post-War) Brotherhood 2pp *Portsmouth City RO*

30340 Portsmouth Players 10pp *Portsmouth City RO*

30341 Portsmouth Referees Society 2pp *Portsmouth City RO*

30342 Southsea (Ladies) Luncheon Club 2pp *Portsmouth City RO*

30343 Metal Box plc, Portsmouth 2pp *Portsmouth City RO*

30344 B Durant, builder and decorator, Southsea 3pp *Portsmouth City RO*

30345 T Cobb & Sons, haulage contractors, Portsmouth 4pp *Portsmouth City RO*

30346 Baker & Son, dispensing chemists and stationers, Cosham 3pp *Portsmouth City RO*

30347 Labour Party: Portsmouth constituency and ward associations 9pp *Portsmouth City RO*

30348 Merionethshire schools 20pp *Gwynedd Archives Service, Dolgellau*

30349 Portsmouth archdeaconry 1p *Portsmouth City RO*

30350 Portsmouth Roman Catholic diocese 2pp *Portsmouth City RO*

30351 Portsmouth: Powerscourt Road Baptist Church 8pp *Portsmouth City RO*

30352 Melrose Abbey charters 8pp *Scottish RO*

30353 Rollo family, Lords Rollo: family and estate corresp and papers 29pp *Scottish RO*

30354 Charles Frederick Gurney Masterman, politician: personal and family corresp and papers 18pp *Birmingham Univ L*

30355 Barber Textile Corporation Ltd, cotton goods mfrs, Bolton 16pp *Lancs RO*

30356 Rotherham: Veiled Victoria Fund 1p *Rotherham Central L*

30357 H Davy's (Exors) Ltd, chemists, Rotherham 3pp *Rotherham Central L*

30358 Gerald E Burgess, architect and surveyor, Dartford 36pp *Kent AO*

30359 Woodhouse & Co, bras founders, Hexthorpe 3pp *Doncaster Archives Dept*

30360 Richard Dunston Ltd, shipbuilders and repairers, Thorne 8pp *Doncaster Archives Dept*

30361 Peglers Ltd, brass founders, Doncaster 12pp *Doncaster Archives Dept*

30362 Yorkshire Brick Co Ltd, Doncaster 4pp *Doncaster Archives Dept*

30363 Gill Brown & Son, auctioneers and valuers, Doncaster 1p *Doncaster Archives Dept*

30364 British Moss Litter Co Ltd, Thorne 5pp *Doncaster Archives Dept*

30365 Wynne-Finch of Voelas, Denbighs: Cefnamwlch, Caerns, estate papers 381pp *Gwynedd Archives Service, Caernarfon*

30366 Wantage and Abingdon Methodist Circuit 7pp *Oxon RO*

30367 Chipping Norton and Stow Methodist Circuit 7pp *Oxon RO*

30368 Suffolk rural deaneries 13pp *Suffolk RO, Ipswich*

30369 Stannington: St Mary's Hospital 22pp *Tyne and Wear Archives Dept*

30370 Todmorden War Memorial Fund Trustees 8pp *Calderdale District Archives*

30371 Wadsworth: Crimsworth Methodist Church 1p *Calderdale District Archives*

30372 Gallery of English Costume, Manchester: MS collection 2pp *Gallery of English Costume, Manchester*

30373 Sir Edward George Clarke, politician and lawyer: corresp and papers 8pp *Private*

30374 Birmingham Markets Committee 5pp *Birmingham Reference L*

30375 Birmingham and Liverpool Ship Canal 20pp *Birmingham Reference L*

30376 Warwickshire schools 9pp *Birmingham Reference L*

30377 Midland Adult Schools Union 4pp *Birmingham Reference L*

30378 Birmingham: Nelson Street Adult Early Morning School 2pp *Birmingham Reference L*

30379 Birmingham Presbytery 1p *Birmingham Reference L*

30380 Southwark Diocesan Council for Wel-Care 132pp *Greater London RO*

30381 Birmingham city 11pp *Birmingham Reference L*

30382 Handsworth Urban District Council 1p *Birmingham Reference L*

30383 Ware of Tilford: family and estate papers 52pp *Surrey RO, Guildford*

30384 Lancaster Methodist Circuit 73pp *Lancs RO*

30385 Ormskirk Methodist Circuit 10pp *Lancs RO*

30386 Joseph Harris Ltd, drycleaners, Birmingham 13pp *Birmingham Reference L*

30387 Birmingham County Football Association 3pp *Birmingham Reference L*

30388 Birmingham Diocesan Lay Readers Board 1p *Birmingham Reference L*

30389 Birmingham: Lord Mayor's War Relief Fund 1p *Birmingham Reference L*

30390 Sydney Arthur Fleming, builder, Hockley 3pp *Birmingham Reference L*

30391 Birmingham Archaeological Society 5pp *Birmingham Reference L*

30392 Midlands Film Theatre Ltd, Birmingham 1p *Birmingham Reference L*

30393 Moseley United Quoit and Bowling Club 1p *Birmingham Reference L*

30394 Liberal Party: Birmingham Association 1p *Birmingham Reference L*

30395 Middlemore Childrens Emigration Homes 30pp *Birmingham Reference L*

30396 Joseph Edward Southall, artist and designer: misc papers 2pp *Birmingham Reference L*

30397 Oliver Banwell, conscientious objector: corresp and papers 2pp *Birmingham Reference L*

30398 Marston Green Cottage Homes 1p *Birmingham Reference L*

30399 Harpur Crewe family, baronets, of Calke Abbey: family and estate papers 525pp *Derbys RO*

30400 Orkney Club, Kirkwall 8pp *Orkney AO*

30401 Orkney Record and Antiquarian Society 13pp *Orkney AO*

30402 George William Reid, schoolmaster: Orkney collections 36pp *Orkney AO*

30403 Philip Augustus Hanrott, solicitor, London: family and business papers 188pp *Greater London RO*

30404 Dublin Mansion House Committee for the Relief of Distress in Ireland 64pp *Dublin Public L*

30405 Caernarfonshire County Council 130pp *Gwynedd Archives Service, Caernarfon*

30406 Conway board of guardians 83pp *Gwynedd Archives Service, Caernarfon*

30407 Conway borough 51pp *Gwynedd Archives Service, Caernarfon*

30408 Wolverhampton Teachers Association 2pp *Wolverhampton Central L*

30409 Wolverhampton Public Libraries Staff Association 1p *Wolverhampton Central L*

30410 Terence John Pitt, MEP: political papers 9pp *Wolverhampton Central L*

30411 Amalgamated Union of Engineering Workers: John Thompson Motor Pressings Ltd works committee, Wolverhampton 1p *Wolverhampton Central L*

30412 Kennedy of Bennane and Kinnarts, Ayrshire: deeds 32pp *Scottish RO*

30413 Sir William Ivor Jennings, professor of law: corresp and papers 19pp *Inst of Commonwealth Studies, London Univ*

30414 Scott of Brotherton, Kincardineshire: deeds 50pp *Scottish RO*

30415 Hay family of Belton, East Lothian: family and estate papers 35pp *Scottish RO*

30416 Maude & Tunnicliffe, solicitors, London: Wynne and Sampson family papers 59pp *Gwynedd Archives Service, Caernarfon*

30417 Castle Eden petty sessions 6pp *Durham RO*

30418 Lanchester, Consett and Stanley petty sessions 11pp *Durham RO*

30419 Seaham petty sessions 5pp *Durham RO*

30420 Chester-le-Street petty sessions 4pp *Durham RO and Tyne and Wear Archives Dept*

30421 Easington petty sessions 2pp *Durham RO*

30422 Dundas of Dundas, West Lothian: family and estate papers 71pp *Scottish RO*

30423 Burnett family of Powis, Aberdeenshire: deeds and estate papers 38pp *Scottish RO*

30424 Carmichael–Anstruther family, baronets, of Anstruther, Fife: deeds and papers 47pp *Scottish RO*

30425 Murray of Lintrose, Perthshire: family and estate papers 96pp *Scottish RO*

30426 Wokingham United Charities 55pp *Berks RO*

30427 Sir Bertram Coghill Alan Windle, anatomist and anthropologist: corresp and papers rel to foundation of Birmingham University 11pp *Birmingham Univ L*

30428 Vaughan Thomas, antiquary: corresp and papers rel to Queen's Hospital, Birmingham 9pp *Birmingham Univ L*

30429 Maidstone Schools Swimming Association 2pp *Kent AO*

30430 Deal Congregational Church 7pp *Kent AO, Folkestone*

30431 Wilson family, baronets, of Eshton Hall: family and estate papers 305pp *Bradford District Archives*

30432 Hythe borough collections 12pp *Private*

30433 Suffolk RO, Lowestoft misc accessions 38pp *Suffolk: RO, Lowestoft*

30434 Rodwell & Co, solicitors, Halesworth: clients papers 6pp *Suffolk RO, Lowestoft*

30435 Long Melford: Holy Trinity Hospital 28pp *Suffolk RO, Bury St Edmunds*

30436 Body, Son & Fleury, surveyors and land agents, Plymouth: clients papers 39pp *Cornwall RO*

30437 Sitwell, Harvey & Money, solicitors, Truro 247pp *Cornwall RO*

30438 Charity Commission: Devon charities accounts 49pp *Devon RO*

30439 Harris family of Hayne: family and estate papers 274pp *Devon RO*

30440 John Stuart Mill, philosopher: letters 3pp *Brotherton L, Leeds Univ*

30441 Sir Edward Alexander Henry (Harry) Legge-Bourke, MP: corresp and papers 36pp *Brotherton L, Leeds Univ*

30442 Strutt family, Barons Belper: family and estate papers 163pp *Notts RO*

30443 Harold Joseph Laski, political scientist: corresp and literary papers 4pp *International Inst of Social History, Amsterdam*

30444 York Minster Library: MS collections 129pp *York Minster L*

30445 Arcade Property Co Ltd, London 4pp *Greater London RO*

30446 Leicestershire petty sessions 2pp *Leics RO*

30447 Fowler and Co, solicitors, Oakham 8pp *Leics RO*

30448 Market Harborough United Industrial and Provident Freehold Land Society 26pp *Leics RO*

30449 Quorn Hunt 28pp *Leics RO*

30450 Gimson and Co Leicester Ltd, engineers 22pp *Leics RO*

30451 G Stibbe & Co, knitwear machinery mfrs, Leicester 2pp *Leics RO*

30452 Woolley, Beardsleys & Bosworth, solicitors, Loughborough 63pp *Leics RO*

30453 Burdett family of Gilmorton: deeds and papers 8pp *Leics RO*

30454 Ashby-de-la-Zouch Methodist Circuit 4pp *Leics RO*

30455 Foxton Baptist Chapel 2pp *Leics RO*

30456 Leicester and South Leicestershire coroners records 11pp *Leics RO*

30457 Caernarvonshire County Constabulary 415pp *Gwynedd Archives Service, Caernarfon*

30458 Caernarvonshire and Anglesey Infirmary 30pp *Gwynedd Archives Service, Caernarfon*

30459 Caernarfon: Castle Square Presbyterian Church 101pp *Gwynedd Archives Service, Caernarfon*

30460 Ivor E Davies, local historian: corresp and papers 43pp *Gwynedd Archives Service, Caernarfon*

30461 Royal Naval Reserve: Caernarfon battery 19pp *Gwynedd Archives Service, Caernarfon*

30462 HM Coastguard: Caernarfon station 11pp *Gwynedd Archives Service, Caernarfon*

30463 Buntingford Rural District Council 12pp *Herts RO*

30464 Hertfordshire United Reformed churches 12pp *Herts RO*

30465 Hertfordshire Unitarian churches 3pp *Herts RO*

30466 Arthur Bulleid, archaeologist and antiquary: corresp and papers 14pp *Somerset RO*

30467 Southwood and Mattock families of Lowton House: family and estate papers 11pp *Somerset RO*

30468 Bridge family of Weston Zoyland: deeds and papers 8pp *Somerset RO*

30469 Wessex Water Authority: Somerset division 68pp *Somerset RO*

30470 Clay & Cocks, solicitors, Nuneaton: clients papers 63pp *Warwicks RO*

30471 Robert William Chapman, English scholar and editor: corresp and papers 25pp *Bodleian L, Oxford*

30472 Townsend family of Wood End House, Medmenham: deeds and family papers 60pp *Bucks RO*

30473 Auckland board of guardians 10pp *Durham RO*

30474 Delap family of Lillingstone Lovell: deeds and estate papers 34pp *Bucks RO*

30475 Grace family of Tring, corn merchants and farmers: business and family papers 19pp *Bucks RO*

30476 William Edward Forster, statesman: corresp and papers 35pp *Trinity Coll L, Dublin*

30477 Robert Childers Barton, politician: corresp and papers 26pp *Trinity Coll L, Dublin*

30478 Brigadier-General Charles Granville Fortescue: diaries 6pp *National Army Mus*

30479 Colonel Sydenham Malthus: corresp and papers 11pp *National Army Mus*

30480 South African War Veterans Association 33pp *National Army Mus*

30481 Clara Collet, civil servant: corresp and papers 12pp *Warwick Univ L*

30482 Confederation of Bank Staff Associations 4pp *Warwick Univ L*

30483 Chadwick Trust 4pp *Univ Coll London*

30484 William James MacKenzie, political scientist: corresp and papers 371pp *Glasgow Univ Archives*

30485 Andrew Browning, historian: corresp and papers 57pp *Glasgow Univ Archives*

30486 John Swinnerton Phillimore, classical scholar: corresp 6pp *Glasgow Univ Archives*

30487 Scottish Temperance Alliance 11pp *Glasgow Univ Archives*

30488 Robert Herbert Story, principal of Glasgow University: corresp and papers 39pp *Glasgow Univ Archives*

30489 Glasgow University Settlement 14pp *Glasgow Univ Archives*

30490 Edward Lionel Gregory Stones, historian: corresp and papers 19pp *Glasgow Univ Archives*

30491 J Millburn & Son, auctioneers and valuers, Aylesbury 12pp *Bucks RO*

30492 John Duncan Mackie, historian: corresp and papers 49pp *Glasgow Univ Archives and St Andrews Univ L*

30493 Harvey family, baronets, of Langley Park: family and estate papers 16pp *Bucks RO*

30494 Sir James Lithgow, 1st Bt, shipbuilder and industrialist: corresp and papers 17pp *Glasgow Univ Archives*

30495 Glasgow Association of University Women 5pp *Glasgow Univ Archives*

30496 Archibald Campbell Craig, chaplain to Glasgow University: corresp and papers 9pp *Private*

30497 Jewish Archives Project, Scotland 7pp *Private*

30498 Hendon board of guardians 10pp *Greater London RO*

30499 Sheffield & Ecclesall Cooperative Society Ltd 8pp *Sheffield Central L*

30500 Salford Museum and Art Gallery: pattern books 2pp *Salford Mus*

30501 Association of Scientific, Technical and Managerial Staffs 98pp *Warwick Univ L*

30502 Paget family, Marquesses of Anglesey: Plas Newydd estate papers 109pp *Univ Coll of N Wales, Bangor*

30503 M MacDonald & Son Ltd, engineers and installers, Renfrew 3pp *Private*

30504 Campbeltown Nursing Society 3pp *Argyll and Bute District Archives*

30505 Ingram Bros (Glasgow) Ltd, bakers 4pp *Private*

30506 Armadale Public House Society Ltd 6pp *Private*

30507 F Johnston & Co Ltd, printers and publishers, Edinburgh 4pp *Private*

30508 Campbell of Jura, Argyllshire: family and estate papers 89pp *Scottish RO*

30509 Carlops and Abbotskerse, Peeblesshire: deeds 34pp *Scottish RO*

30510 JGB Henderson: Linlithgow deeds and papers 88pp *Scottish RO*

30511 Fergusson of Craigdarroch, Dumfriesshire: family and estate papers 32pp *Scottish RO*

30512 Hunter of Barjarg, Dumfries-shire: family and estate papers 25pp *Scottish RO*

30513 Perth: King James VI Hospital 110pp *Scottish RO*

30514 Makgill family, baronets, of Fingask and Kemback: family and estate papers 67pp *Scottish RO*

30515 Ramsay family, baronets, of Bamff, Perthshire: family and estate papers 83pp *Scottish RO*

30516 George Eland, local historian: corresp and papers 1p *Bucks RO*

30517 National Farmers Union: Cheshire branch 7pp *Cheshire RO*

30518 Birmingham Unitarian Brotherly Benefit Society 2pp *Birmingham Reference L*

30519 Northwich Urban District Council 1p *Cheshire RO*

30520 Oakmere Hospital 2pp *Cheshire RO*

30521 Dutton Hospital 2pp *Cheshire RO*

30522 East Cheshire Group Hospital Management Committee 4pp *Cheshire RO*

30523 Great Warford: Mary Dendy Hospital 7pp *Cheshire RO*

30524 Florence Nightingale: letters 16pp *Wellcome Inst*

30525 Smith & Wiseman, cotton spinners, Colne 9pp *Lancs RO*

30526 Hetton Race Co Ltd and Houghton Greyhound Stadium Club 5pp *Tyne and Wear Archives Dept*

30527 Chopwell: Trinity Methodist Church 1p *Tyne and Wear Archives Dept*

30528 Marley Hill and Blackhall Mill Wesleyan Methodist chapels 3pp *Tyne and Wear Archives Dept*

30529 British Radiofrequency Spectroscopy Group 5pp *Nottingham Univ L*

30530 Thomas Smith's Stamping Works (Coventry) Ltd, drop forgers 2pp *Coventry City RO*

30531 D Blakemore & Son Ltd, sheet metal mfrs, Coventry 3pp *Coventry City RO*

30532 William Franklin & Son Ltd, ribbon mfrs, Coventry 1p *Coventry City RO*

30533 Daimler Motor Co Ltd, motor mfrs, Coventry 13pp *Coventry City RO*

30534 Alfred Herbert Ltd, machine tool mfrs, Coventry 2pp *Coventry City RO*

30535 J & J Cash Ltd, ribbon and tape mfrs, Coventry 15pp *Coventry City RO*

30536 Edwards The Printers Ltd, Coventry 8pp *Coventry City RO*

30537 Willans family of Dolforgan, Montgomeryshire: deeds and estate papers 150pp *National L of Wales*

30538 Mackay family, Barons Reay: family and estate papers 145pp *Scottish RO*

30539 Nasmith family: Hamilton deeds and papers 104pp *Scottish RO*

30540 Sir William Fraser, antiquary: deeds and papers collection 950pp *Scottish RO*

30541 Egerton family, Barons Egerton of Tatton: family and estate papers 3pp *John Rylands Univ L of Manchester*

30542 Stroud and District Nursing Association 3pp *Glos RO*

30543 Electrical Association for Women: Dursley and district branch 1p *Glos RO*

30544 Coleford United Reformed Church 5pp *Glos RO*

30545 Williams-Wynn family, baronets, of Wynnstay, Denbighs: family and estate papers 743pp *National L of Wales*

30546 Duke of Edinburgh's Royal Regiment (Berkshire and Wilt-shire) 138pp *Private*

30547 Gloucestershire rural district councils 11pp *Glos RO*

30548 London Society for the Promotion of Christianity among the Jews: Irish auxiliary 2pp *Representative Church Body L, Dublin*

30549 Church Missionary Society Ireland 4pp *Representative Church Body L, Dublin*

30550 Elphin: Bishop Hodson's Endowment and Grammar School 3pp *Representative Church Body L, Dublin*

30551 Hugh Jackson Lawlor, dean of St Patrick's, Dublin: corresp and papers 8pp *Representative Church Body L, Dublin*

30552 Protestant Orphan Society for the County of Sligo 4pp *Representative Church Body L, Dublin*

30553 J Arthurs, antiquary: autograph collection 138pp *Glamorgan RO*

30554 Cardiganshire Liberal Association 19pp *National L of Wales*

30555 Sir Barnes Wallis, aeronautical engineer: corresp and papers 94pp *Science Mus L*

30556 SP Bevon, solicitor, Wrexham 39pp *Clwyd RO, Ruthin*

30557 Prince of Wales Dry Dock Co, Swansea, Ltd 12pp *Glamorgan RO*

30558 London: St John's Hospital 10pp *Greater London RO*

30559 London: Royal Eye Hospital 43pp *Greater London RO*

30560 London: South Western Hospital 4pp *Greater London RO*

30561 London: Holmhurst Home 2pp *Greater London RO*

30562 Amelia Opie, novelist and poet: letters 8pp *Huntington L, San Marino, California, USA*

30563 Lambeth Group Hospital Management Committee 2pp *Greater London RO*

30564 Trecastle Estate: deeds and papers 294pp *Glamorgan RO*

30565 Robinson David & Co, timber dealers, Cardiff 4pp *Glamorgan RO*

30566 Baring Brothers & Co, merchant bankers: MS collections 57pp *Private*

30567 Bouverie-Pusey family of Pusey: family and estate papers 47pp *Berks RO*

30568 Macgregor Laird, shipowner: letters to his wife 26pp *National Mus on Merseyside*

30569 Robert James Loyd-Lindsay, Baron Wantage: corresp and papers 106pp *Private*

30570 Woking Magistrates Court 1p *Surrey RO, Kingston*

30571 William Powell Price, solicitor, Brecon: clients papers 31pp *Powys Archives*

30572 Jeffreys and Powell, solicitors, Brecon: clients papers 200pp *Powys Archives*

30573 Williams family of Penpont, Brecon: Abercamlais deeds and estate papers 150pp *Powys Archives*

30574 W Haswell & Son, masonry contractors, Chester 17pp *Chester City RO*

30575 Bridewell Museum, Norwich: textile industry collection 4pp *Bridewell Mus, Norwich*

30576 Society of the Holy Trinity, Ascot Priory, Berks 9pp *Private*

30577 Capell family, Earls of Essex: deeds and estate papers 1p *Norfolk RO*

30578 Powell family of Horton Old Hall: family and estate papers 21pp *Bradford District Archives*

30579 Coke family, Earls of Leicester: Ashill, Panworth Hall and Saham Toney estate papers 3pp *Norfolk RO*

30580 Dunlop Rubber Co Ltd 21pp *Greater London RO*

30581 English Table Tennis Association 16pp *Liverpool Univ Archives*

30582 Arnold Bennett, novelist and playwright: corresp and misc papers 6pp *Keele Univ L*

30583 Sheffield Diocesan Education Committee 1p *Sheffield Central L*

30584 Elstead Congregational Church 7pp *Surrey RO, Guildford*

30585 Godalming United Reformed Church 22pp *Surrey RO, Guildford*

30586 Milford United Reformed Church 2pp *Surrey RO, Guildford*

30587 James Luck, blacksmith, Milford: business and family papers 8pp *Surrey RO, Guildford*

30588 Cobham Combined Charities 3pp *Surrey RO, Guildford*

30589 Abel-Smith family of Wendover: deeds and estate papers 7pp *Bucks RO*

30590 Sutcliffe family of Heptonstall: deeds and papers 14pp *Calderdale District Archives*

30591 JC Bottomley & Emerson Ltd, paint and dye mfrs, Brighouse 4pp *Calderdale District Archives*

30592 S Appleyard & Co, machine tool makers, Halifax 5pp *Calderdale District Archives*

30593 Sir Charles Stewart Addis, international banker: corresp and papers 158pp *School of Oriental and African Studies, London Univ*

30594 Pakenham family, Earls of Longford: family and estate papers 48pp *Private*

30595 Turvey Congregational Church 24pp *Beds RO*

30596 Luton Water Co 26pp *Beds RO*

30597 Bedfordshire Citizens Advice Bureau 11pp *Beds RO*

30598 Simplex Mechanical Handling Co Ltd, Bedford 8pp *Beds RO*

30599 White family of Corhams Manor: deeds and manorial records 39pp *Bucks RO*

30600 Tow Law Presbyterian Church 3pp *Durham RO*

30601 Easington District Council 2pp *Durham RO*

30602 Bedfordshire schools 5pp *Various locations*

30603 Danson family of Liverpool: corresp and pa ers 100pp *National Mus on Merseyside*

30604 Association of Education Committees 5pp *Brotherton L, Leeds Univ*

30605 Frederick Meyrick, rector of Blickling, Norfolk: corresp 24pp *Pusey House, Oxford*

30606 Thomas E Morris, vicar of Carleton, Yorks: corresp and papers 23pp *Pusey House, Oxford*

30607 Edmund S Ffoulkes, vicar of St Mary the Virgin, Oxford: corresp 13pp *Pusey House, Oxford*

30608 William Pleydell-Bouverie, 3rd Earl of Radnor: corresp 13pp *Pusey House, Oxford*

30609 Lower Strafforth and Tickhill petty sessions 41pp *Doncaster Archives Dept*

30610 Doncaster petty sessions 16pp *Doncaster Archives Dept*

Principal replacements of and additions to existing reports included:

1108 Ferrand of St Ives and Harden Grange, Yorks: family and estate papers 250pp *Bradford District Archives*

4634 Bulwer of Heydon: family and estate papers 122pp *Norfolk RO*

★5033 Rogers of Penrose: family and estate papers 141pp *Cornwall RO and Private*

6790 William Henry Lytton Earle Bulwer, Baron Dalling and Bulwer: diplomatic corresp and papers 128pp *Norfolk RO*

7865 Scottish Catholic Archives: MS collections 2900pp *Scottish Catholic Archives*

10568 Chirk Castle MSS 1270pp *National L of Wales*

12332 Coke family, Earls of Leicester: estate papers, various counties (Holkham MSS) 187pp *Private*

17164 Ramsay family, Earls of Dalhousie: family and estate papers 1,009pp *Scottish RO*

★19000 Hill family, baronets, of Brook Hall, co Londonderry: family and estate papers 45pp *PRO of N Ireland*

★19292 Saumarez family, Barons de Saumarez: family and estate papers 1527pp *Suffolk RO Ipswich*

★20078 William King, archbishop of Dublin: corresp (Lyons collection) 820pp *Trinity Coll L, Dublin*

22080 Herbert family, Earls of Pembroke: family and estate papers 91pp *Wilts RO and Private*

★26129 Thomas Edward Ellis, politician: corresp and papers 271pp *National L of Wales*

Index to Repositories in Part I

Printed in the United Kingdom for Her Majesty's Stationery Office
Dd 0289357   C8   9/88